FELICIA CARTRIGHT
AND THE CASE OF THE
FRIGHTENED STUDENT

Felicia
Joan

FELICIA CARTRIGHT

AND THE CASE OF THE
FRIGHTENED STUDENT

BERNARD PALMER

ANEKO
PRESS

Aneko Press Youth

www.anekopress.com

Aneko Press, Life Sentence Publishing, and our logos are trademarks of Life Sentence Publishing, Inc.
203 E. Birch Street
P.O. Box 652
Abbotsford, WI 54405

JUVENILE FICTION / Religious / Christian / Action & Adventure

Paperback ISBN: 979-8-88936-290-6

eBook ISBN: 979-8-88936-291-3

10 9 8 7 6 5 4 3 2 1

Available where books are sold

CONTENTS

CHAPTER 1

REGULATIONS, AND THEN SOME

It was fall. The wind was whipping across the campus at Wellington School for Girls. It sent the leaves cascading down from the great oaks, beeches, and maples and rattled windows in the gray, forbidding buildings. Rain had been threatening all day; now, at dusk, the sidewalks were moist, and some drops spattered the screens.

Felicia Cartright stood at the window of her room and looked out. She was a small girl, with blond hair and dainty features. A smiling, bright-eyed girl, she was as popular with the faculty as she was with her classmates. But now, as she looked out at the growing darkness, she hugged herself and shivered.

"Br-r-r," she said to herself. "It looks cold outside."

"Turn up the heat," her roommate suggested.

Joan Bailey was sprawled carelessly across the bed reading a book.

"That won't help any." Felicia turned back. "I was just thinking of how cold it's going to be this winter. And from the looks of the weather tonight, it isn't going to be long until we'll have a foot of snow."

Joan closed her book and sat up. She was taller than Felicia, with dark hair and a quick, impetuous manner.

"It doesn't bother me at all," she said. "I'm immune to it."

"Who was doing all the complaining last winter about snow and cold?" Felicia asked, scoffing.

"It's not going to bother me a bit. Compared to the cold blast Miss Duncan gives every time she calls me into her office to talk about my grades, a blizzard is a little spring zephyr."

The other girl laughed.

"You could take care of that easily," she replied.

"And just what would you suggest doing?" Joan demanded. "I think Miss Duncan comes into her office every morning, rings for her secretary, and says, 'Check Miss Bailey's grades.'"

"If it bothers you that much, you could put a stop to it just by studying a little."

Joan made a face at her. "You would have to mention studying and spoil my evening."

Felicia went back to her desk and sat down. She still had an English report to write.

"Did you see what enrolled this afternoon?" Joan asked.

Felicia shook her head.

"I don't know her name, but she was wrapped in designer clothes and delivered to us in a big black limousine a block and a half long."

"She must be the one the girls were talking about at dinner. I think her dad is a big industrialist or a politician or something."

"He's something," Joan replied, "you can be sure. You should see her, Felicia. She came waltzing up the steps as though she owned Wellington. She's going to be a real prize. I can't imagine her staying very long. I don't think she's 'Wellington timbre,' to quote our beloved Miss Duncan."

"Have you met her yet, Joan?"

The other girl shook her dark head. "And from what I've seen of her, I don't think that either one of us would enjoy the ordeal."

"If you don't know her, Joan," Felicia asked simply, "why are you so sure that you wouldn't like her?"

Joan put her book aside.

"I deserved that, Felicia," she said. "I guess you have to remind me of my Christian responsibilities once in a while."

"I didn't mean it that way, Joan," the fair-haired girl answered. "But I keep thinking of the way Christ changed my life."

"And mine," Joan broke in.

"And yours," Felicia acknowledged. "And I realize how he could change this new girl's life – if she would only put her trust in Him."

"Unless I'm badly mistaken, she doesn't put her trust in anyone or anything except herself and her dad's money."

"The poor girl," Felicia said thoughtfully.

The new girl was assigned to a room next to theirs, so they were introduced to her. They learned that her name was Wendy Adams; her dad was an important judge and a figure in state politics. She had briefly attended two other exclusive girls' schools.

"I couldn't stand their ridiculous regulations," she told Joan and Felicia airily. "I packed up my things and went home. I don't do anything that I don't want to do."

"You didn't better yourself any when it comes to regulations," Joan told her pointedly. "We've got all the regulations any other school has and then some."

"But they're really good regulations," Felicia added, "and it's no trouble to keep them."

"Well, I told Dad that I'd come, but I wouldn't promise to stay." She was taller than most girls at Wellington, but she carried herself with grace and dignity, without concern that she was tall. In fact, she seemed to glory in it, looking down on the other girls. Her clothes were the latest fashion and expensive. The girls soon learned that her temper matched the red in her hair. It was quite apparent that she usually got her way.

"It's really nice here, Wendy," Joan said, "if you try to like it."

She smiled sardonically.

"We'll see."

One week passed, then another. The cold weather Felicia had been predicting gave way to the warmth of Indian summer. The nights were crisp and cool, but the days basked in the rays of a lingering sun.

Wendy went from one class to another, indifferently, studying if the mood seized her. She came to meals when she felt like it and rebelled at the early morning bell and at the lights-out bell at 10:30 p.m.

"They actually expect us to get up at that heathenish hour!" she exclaimed. "Why it's practically in the middle of the night. And we have to go to bed like children. I tell you, it's driving me crazy."

"You're talking to the wrong ones," Joan said, laughing. "Go down and see Miss Duncan. She is the one who rings the bells."

Wendy flounced across her dormitory room and dropped into a chair in front of Felicia and Joan.

"I don't care what the regulations are," she retorted, bristling hotly. "I've got to get out for a weekend and have some fun. If you two won't help me, I'll do it alone."

"'Said the little red hen,'" Joan Bailey murmured.

Wendy whirled to face her.

"Now what did you say?" she demanded. "I don't like the laugh."

"It was just a private little joke of mine that probably wasn't funny," Joan said with a careless wave of her hand. "The jokes I tell usually aren't. So skip it."

Wendy pulled impulsively at the expensive bracelet on her arm.

"I can't stand it here another long, dreary weekend," she said. "I'll die if I have to spend another Sunday in this morgue. I want a straight answer from you. Are you going to help me?"

"If you're still trying to talk us into helping you break regulations," Felicia said, "I'm afraid that we won't be able to help you."

"Besides," Joan added firmly, "you haven't had an encounter with 'Eagle Eye' Duncan yet. She knows all the tricks that you know and about forty dozen besides. Nobody–nobody fools her."

"Then you just don't want to help me," she retorted, pouting. "That's all."

"We want to help you," Felicia said. "We don't want to help you get into trouble. Miss Duncan is positively uncanny when it comes to smelling out infraction of rules. You'll be asking for trouble by sneaking out."

"Trouble?" Joan echoed. "Miss Duncan will draw and quarter you if she finds that you've left the campus without permission. That rule is in big, red letters on her desk. That's one thing that just isn't done at Wellington."

Her voice rose, and her green eyes flashed.

"I might be new here," Wendy snapped, "but I can tell you this much. I'm not afraid of Miss Duncan. She doesn't scare me at all."

"She ought to," Joan said sternly. "She's got all the rest of us scared."

That was something of an exaggeration. Miss Duncan, Dean of Women at the exclusive Wellington School for Girls was strict but very fair.

As she always said: "It is my responsibility to be strict. That is why I am paid my salary. At Wellington, each young woman assumes full responsibility for her conduct. They learn how to take care of themselves, to respect authority, and to know the purpose and meaning of restraint."

Actually, Miss Duncan loved her girls and was most concerned about them. Only a few days before, she had called Felicia Cartright and Joan Bailey into her office to talk with them about the newcomer.

She nodded icily to the girls when they came in, asked them to close the door and be seated. They did so uneasily, eyeing her with concern.

"You know, of course," she began, folding her well-manicured hands, "that you must treat this conversation in strict confidence. It must not leave the confines of this room or the three of us."

They both nodded.

"But if it's about not having our lights out last night after hours," Joan broke in, "that was my fault. Felicia was in bed and half asleep. She had nothing to do with it."

Miss Duncan's expression did not change.

"I surmised as much. I was just checking my calendar for tomorrow. You are scheduled to see me about that incident after lunch, Miss Bailey. At the moment I have another matter that I wish to talk with you about."

The girls looked at one another strangely.

"I wish to talk with you about Miss Adams."

Joan Bailey sighed wearily.

"That drip," she exclaimed. "I might have known."

"Miss Bailey," the Dean of Women replied acidly, "a cultured, well-bred, Wellington young lady never refers to another as a-a drip." She rolled the word off her tongue gingerly, as though even to speak it was distasteful.

"I'm sorry," Joan said quickly. "I really didn't mean it. But Wendy Adams is so sour and disagreeable that none of the girls like her."

"Precisely." Miss Duncan leaned forward. "Miss Adams has never had to put herself in the discipline we at Wellington find best. That is why I wanted to talk with you and Miss Cartright. As you probably already know, Miss Adams is the daughter of a wealthy and powerful political figure in New Hampshire. She comes to us with very good recommendations.

What is equally important, she is capable of doing excellent work."

"What is it that you want us to do?" Felicia asked.

"I'm coming to that. Unfortunately, for all her good attributes, Miss Adams is not finding herself at Wellington. She finds regulations difficult. She is holding herself aloof from the other students in a way that is gaining her their dislike. She scoffs at Wellington tradition. I am very much afraid that unless something is done, and quickly, we may be forced to dismiss her. That would be a tragedy."

"I've noticed how she is," Felicia replied, a warm smile briefly lighting her dainty features.

Few people thought Felicia pretty the first time they saw her. As they got acquainted and came to know her better, they thought of her as beautiful. Her smile was as quick and ready as her manner was kind. She seemed drawn, as though by some invisible radar, to the heartsick, the lonely, any who needed help. From the moment that she set foot on Wellington Campus everyone recognized that, somehow, she was different than most of the other girls. Now her face was giving evidence of sympathetic interest.

"I feel sorry for her," she said.

The Dean of Women took a few moments before going on.

"Miss Adams quite obviously finds it difficult to adjust to the regulations here at Wellington. I am quite sure that she has found it difficult to accept the restraint of regulations. From observing her, I should judge that perhaps she has had her own way at home." Miss Duncan leaned forward and pointed with her pencil. "You girls have both made a good adjustment here. In a way you symbolize the spirit of Wellington."

"I hope she remembers that when she calls me in here tomorrow," Joan thought.

Miss Duncan fastened her gaze on Joan. She could not have known what Joan thought. But, knowing the merry, bright-eyed girl, she might have guessed.

"In spite of some carelessness on your part, Miss Bailey," she added, "about studying and obeying certain regulations, both of you have been able to fit yourselves into the Wellington way and to show very good progress and adjustment. Of all the girls here at Wellington, I believe that you two are the most apt to be able to help her."

"We'll certainly try," Felicia said quickly.

"You will be performing a real service both to the school and to Miss Adams." Miss Duncan reached for a sheaf of papers and began to go through them. That was her standard signal that the interview had ended.

In the hall, Joan turned to her companion.

"There's one thing I'd like to know," she said. "Why is it that you and I get called on for jobs like this?"

"Maybe we *can* help Wendy," Felicia said. "That's the important thing. She's so very unhappy."

CHAPTER 2

WENDY REJECTS HER FRIENDS' INTEREST

Felicia Cartright and Joan Bailey went upstairs arm in arm.

"Am I glad that's over!" Joan exclaimed. "I thought Miss Duncan was going to give us the third degree."

"A guilty conscience?" Felicia teased, laughing. "Every time Miss Duncan wants to see us, you think trouble."

"And I've got good reason. Most every time she wants to see me, it *is* trouble."

They went into their room, and Felicia closed the door.

"I only hope we can help that poor, unhappy girl. She seems to be so miserable."

"Unhappy isn't the word for it," Joan retorted bluntly.

"Miss Duncan seemed to think so."

"The only thing wrong with Wendy Adams is that she's spoiled, s-p-o-i-l-e-d. She's Judge Adams' daughter. He's that famous trial judge in New Hampshire. They've got so much money that she uses silver shoe trees and gold coat hangers, and I think she's got diamonds for buttons."

Felicia laughed. "Joan," she exclaimed, "you're impossible!"

"Well, that might be exaggeration, but I can tell you this much. She's loaded. And she won't let any of us forget it. The other day she informed me that there has never been a time in her life when she wanted something that her dad hadn't rushed to get for her. She's had so much that nothing's exciting anymore."

Felicia Cartright's face grew serious.

"The poor girl," she said, "I feel so terribly sorry for her."

Joan's eyes softened.

"I guess I feel sorry for her, too," she said. "The other girls do resent her and do a good job of leaving her alone. I don't think that she's got a friend in Wellington."

"We've got to do what we can for her."

It had been very easy for Joan and Felicia to make friends with Wendy Adams. She had not been at school long, and, although everyone had to take part in certain activities, she didn't do more than the school required. She was so disagreeable that her roommate, a girl from her hometown, got tired of her before the end of the second week and talked Miss Duncan into moving her to another room.

Wendy pretended not to care.

"It doesn't make any difference to me whether I've a roommate or not," she said defensively, with a toss of her head. "I'm about fed up with this school anyway. The girls here are positively stupid."

Joan Bailey bristled. She would have retorted sharply, but Felicia smiled and spoke first.

"I think they're really not that way, Wendy," she answered mildly. "And I'm sure that you agree. We have a nice group of girls at Wellington, if only you'd get to know them."

For a minute, Wendy Adams stood there scanning their faces with her eyes. Pain lurked behind the sham of indifference. Pain that went deep.

"All right." Her voice was brittle and harsh. "I want to know the truth. What's the matter? What's wrong with me? Why is it that nobody likes me?"

Felicia and Joan glanced at one another.

"Did the girls tell you that they don't like you?" the Cartright girl asked gently.

"I don't have to be told. I know that they don't like me. Why do they treat me as they do? What have I done that makes me undesirable?"

Joan Bailey answered. The acid was gone from her tongue. She spoke as kindly as Felicia had ever heard her.

"There's another question that you ought to ask

yourself, Wendy, if you haven't done so. Just how friendly have you been to the other girls since you came here?"

Wendy straightened haughtily, and her mouth firmed.

"Maybe I haven't been too friendly," she said. "I'm quite particular about my friends. Frankly, I haven't met anyone at Wellington that I'd care to have as a friend." She pulled out a chair and sat down in it regally. "Excepting you two, of course," she added quickly.

Felicia studied her. There was a pampered, sophisticated look about her; a look that spelled boredom. But more than that, her pretty face, especially her eyes, reflected loneliness.

"Joan and I will be praying for you, Wendy," she said at last.

Wendy Adams started at the thought, and there was resentment and defiance in her manner.

"Praying for me?" she echoed. What makes you so sure that *I* need to have someone pray for me, Felicia Cartright? I'll have you know that I can take care of myself without any help. You can save your praying for someone who needs and appreciates it." She now spoke hotly, as though Felicia had insulted her.

"I didn't intend to offend you," the Cartright girl assured her. "But since I've become a Christian and put my trust in Jesus Christ, I have come to see that He holds the answer to all problems, regardless of what they are. I have learned that from personal experience."

"And so have I," Joan added. "When I first came to Wellington, I had some of the same problems that you're having. It was so hard for me to fit into the discipline we have here. I couldn't get used to having to eat on schedule, having to get up and go to bed at a certain hour, having to study whether I needed to study or not."

In spite of herself, Felicia snickered.

"Go ahead and laugh," Joan retorted. "There are times when I don't need to study. When I first came here, you know that I had trouble getting adjusted."

"I'm sorry. I remember what it was like when you came, Joan."

"So do I," she went on. "Until I put my trust in Jesus Christ, I was lonely and so terribly unhappy."

"Well, I'm not," Wendy retorted hotly. "I want you to know that I'm having a ball here. A real ball! In spite of this school with its miserable regulations and its girls!"

"The most important thing any of us can ever do in this life," Felicia continued, "is to recognize that we're sinners, to see that we're deep in sin, to confess our sin, and put our trust in Christ to save us, yes, from ourselves." She paused and leaned forward earnestly. "If you would only try Him, Wendy, you would see what a great difference Christ can make in your life."

The other girl looked at her then kind of snorted derisively.

"I might have known there would be something like this when you two started being nice," she said, forcing herself to laugh mirthlessly. "I figured that there would be a catch, a sermon. Your kind usually have to do something like that." Her voice began rising. "Well, I can tell you right now that you'd just as well save your breath. Go back and tell Miss Duncan that your preaching doesn't impress me. I'm not going to go religious, and I'm not buying this kind of friendship."

Felicia thought that Wendy's eyes were unspeakably sad.

"We didn't intend to preach," Joan tried to explain.

"That's a laugh!" Wendy snapped. "The only reason you've been nice to me has been so that you'd have a chance to blast me at intervals with religion. Well, you'd just as well quit! You're wasting my time and yours!" She got to her feet and stormed to the window where she stood for a moment or two, staring out past the fire escape at the dark buildings across the campus. The wind whistling through the trees caught her attention. She listened to it. Again she spoke defiantly. "I don't care whether I've got any friends at Wellington or not!"

CHAPTER 3

A FACE AT THE WINDOW

Joan and Felicia didn't stay too long in Wendy's room.

"Now that was an outburst," Joan said when they were alone again. "I didn't know anyone could be so bitter."

Felicia pushed books aside and sat down at the desk.

"I can tell you this," the Bailey girl went on. "You were right about Wendy being unhappy. She's miserable."

"And so bitter. She's bitter and miserable, Joan."

"We'll have to be careful to pray regularly for her."

The girls did continue to pray for Wendy Adams, but it began to appear they were not going to get another opportunity to talk with her about Jesus again. She studiously avoided them. If they came into a room, Wendy made it a point to leave if at all possible. At mealtime, if they chanced to sit near her, she talked incessantly and fast, giving them no opportunity to mention anything spiritual.

The weekend that she wanted to go to Boston came and passed. She sulked in her room most of the time. She let everyone know what she thought of Miss Duncan for refusing to give her a pass. Still, she made no effort to break regulations by slipping off without a pass.

"At least she didn't try to sneak out," Joan said. "That's one thing in her favor."

Felicia remained silent.

"But she's so distant," she finally said. "She's so withdrawn. If only she would let us talk with her. If only she could see what Christ can and would do in her life."

It was more than a week later before Felicia Cartright found an opportunity to talk with Wendy. It came quickly and so unexpectedly that it startled her. She was sitting alone at her desk, trying to outline an English theme. There was a faint knock at the door, and the Adams girl came in.

"I saw Joan go down to the lounge," Wendy observed as she entered, "so I knew that you were alone, Felicia."

Felicia smiled. "Joan is going to go to town to the city library. She won't be back for a couple of hours."

Wendy crossed the room and sat down. She was tall and stately, dressed in the latest fashion.

"I'm sorry that I was so rude to you and Joan the other night. I was upset."

"That's quite all right. We understand."

Wendy's cheeks colored. She was not used to apologizing to anyone.

"And I'm sorry that I ridiculed your–your faith. As my father says, religion is a very personal matter. We must be tolerant of each other's religious beliefs and not interfere with them."

Felicia waited. "I'm glad you came to see me this evening," she said gently.

"You did get me thinking when you mentioned praying for me." She clasped her hands tightly. "We've never paid much attention to religion in our home."

A couple of girls were laughing and talking as they went by in the hall. Wendy waited until they had passed Felicia's door.

"Oh," she went on, "Dad always has a Bible in his study, and there were several times when I found him reading it. But he always said that he didn't believe that parents should force religion on their children. So neither he nor Mom ever urged us to go to Sunday school or church."

Felicia reached for her Bible. "Did you have any particular question?" she asked.

Wendy appeared uncomfortable. "I–I don't know," she said. "It was just a silly idea of mine. I'm sorry now that I brought it up. Skip it."

"I thought perhaps there was something that was disturbing you."

"I've been watching you and Joan," Wendy continued. "You are different from most of the others here."

"What do you mean?"

"Oh," she went on, "you seem to have as much fun as the other girls and all of that, but there's something solid about you. It may be silly, but I just got to wondering what it is that makes you different." She paused and leaned forward. "Could it possibly be your religion?"

Felicia Cartright smiled. "If Joan and I are different," she said, "it's not because of anything that we've done in our own strength. It is because of Jesus and what He has done in our lives."

"That's what I don't understand."

"We've acknowledged the fact that we are sinners, confessed our sin, and put our trust in Christ who can forgive sin and save us from sin's punishment," Felicia said. "That's the first thing. Then we committed our lives to Christ."

She opened her Bible to one passage of Scripture after another, explaining to Wendy how sin came into the world and how God sent Jesus Christ so that we might be saved. She explained how a person must recognize that he is a sinner and needs salvation, that he must confess his sin and put his trust in Jesus.

"I've known of Christ, of course," Wendy said wonderingly. "I've always thought of Him as great, a noble example and teacher. But this whole idea of redemption is something new to me. I've never heard it. It's fascinating."

"It is fascinating," Felicia continued, "because it presents each one of us with a means of reaching heaven. The Bible tells us we can't be good enough to be worthy of heaven. But God, through Christ, provides a way."

For a long minute, Wendy was silent. The defiance was gone, at least momentarily, from her eyes. Felicia watched her and prayed silently. At last, she glanced at her watch and rose quickly.

"Oh," she exclaimed, "I've got to run! I'll see you and talk about this another time."

When Joan returned later, Felicia told her about the visit.

"It's hard to believe that there are people right here in America who have never heard the gospel, isn't it?" Joan said.

"But the girl is so mixed up."

* * *

There was a flurry of excitement at the school the following morning when the Boston news came on.

"Oh, look!" someone squealed, pointing to the headlines. "Wendy's father is the judge who's trying that racketeer."

Wendy Adams managed a twisted, superior little

smile. "Rocky Gallardo?" she asked. "I've known about it for weeks."

"But doesn't it frighten you?"

"Why should it?"

"They say that he's in narcotics and smuggling and rackets and that he's even been responsible for three or four killings. He's boasted that no judge would ever sentence him and live long."

She shrugged her shoulders. "He's never before been brought up before my father."

"Just the same, it would scare me." The girl shuddered. "I don't think I would be able to sleep nights. Just imagine! Having to try a man like that!"

For a week the news played up the Gallardo case, and for the first time, Wendy began to achieve a kind of popularity at Wellington. Girls who had not known that she was Judge Adams' daughter and had snubbed her pointedly now went out of their way to be nice to her.

"I'm glad that Wendy's getting acquainted with some of the girls and making a few friends," Felicia said, "but I've been trying for a week to talk with her alone. There's always a crowd around her."

Felicia was surprised and happy when Wendy sought her out that night in the cafeteria.

"Could you come to my room for a few minutes this evening?" Wendy asked. She smiled. "There's something I want to talk with you about."

Felicia finished eating and went prayerfully to Wendy's room.

"I didn't expect you so soon." Wendy crossed to her desk, picked up a letter, and returned it to the envelope.

"You acted concerned, so I came as soon as I could," the Cartright girl said.

"I'm not, really." She went to the window, raised the shade absent-mindedly, and looked out on the fire escape. "I mean no more than usual." She sat down at the desk and began to toy with the letter. "Your talk with me the other night was disturbing. I decided that I ought to go home and talk with Mom and Dad."

"A decision for the Savior must be between you and Him," Felicia reminded her. "Each one of us must face the sin question personally and answer it personally."

"Dad is a judge and a very wise man. I trust his advice."

"What of the advice of the Bible?" the Cartright girl asked. "It says, *You must be born again.*"

Wendy's face darkened. "I've got to work this out in my way."

Felicia tried to conceal her disappointment.

"I wrote Mom and told her that I had a difficult problem to solve," the other girl continued. "This afternoon I heard from her." Now she opened the letter and began to read.

You know that we always want you to come home whenever you can, Wendy. But if you have a problem, I hope that you won't disturb your father with it right at this time. He is trying the Gallardo case and is very disturbed about it. In cases like this, there is always the danger that something might happen to cause a mistrial. Because of that, he's giving the trial his full attention right now.

I don't feel that it is wise to trouble him with personal matters.

Love,

Mom

"What is it that you wanted to talk with me about?" Felicia asked.

"I intended to go over the matter with Dad, but I don't want to bother him now. So I thought I would ask you to go over the entire matter again from the beginning so I can get it straight in my mind."

"Why, certainly."

Felicia paused, groping for words.

In that instant, Wendy Adams screamed.

"Felicia!" she cried, her voice shrill and quavering with fright. "Felicia!" She was pointing a trembling finger toward the window.

Felicia Cartright gasped. For an instant, she did not speak.

Girls in adjoining rooms came scurrying down the hall and pounded on the door.

"What's wrong? What's going on in there?"

"What is it, Wendy?" Felicia asked.

"I–I saw a man's face at the window."

The girls at the door were still pounding. Felicia went to let them in. They came piling into the room. "W-w-what's happening?" they wanted to know.

"I–I saw him," Wendy repeated numbly.

"Are you sure you saw someone at the window?" Felicia said. "Why would anyone do that?"

"I–I don't know," she went on. "I saw the top of his head first. Then he raised up and stared through the window right at me."

CHAPTER 4

GOING HOME FOR WHAT?

By this time, someone had summoned Miss Duncan. She came into the room with studied calmness. The girls fell back silently to make way.

"Felicia," she said, her voice crisp and firm, "may I ask what is going on here?"

There was no doubt about her disapproval. A Wellington girl did not disrupt routine by screaming.

Hurriedly they told her what had happened. Miss Duncan's expression did not change. She turned to the students who had crowded into Wendy's room.

"You may return to your rooms," she said. "We will have the authorities here in a few moments, so there is no cause for alarm."

"Go back to my room after what just happened?" someone echoed, horrified. "I'd die!"

"Miss Jenkins," the Dean of Women said calmly,

"a Wellington girl never loses her poise. You will be quite safe, I can assure you."

Miss Duncan started for the door.

"Miss Cartright and Miss Adams, come with me. The officers will undoubtedly wish to question both of you."

"Miss Duncan," Wendy began when they were in the office on the main floor and the door was securely closed, "must you call the authorities?"

"Most assuredly. Wellington School property has been violated, and we have more than two hundred girls in our care. We have a certain responsibility to the parents of all." Then she saw the look on the Adams girl's face. "Is there any reason why I shouldn't?"

She sat down at her desk and motioned the girls to chairs across from her.

"My father is trying the Rocky Gallardo case," Wendy said, "and is very concerned in case the defense might try to delay it again by having it declared a mistrial. If the papers find out about this, some reporter is sure to try to connect me with that. It might be enough to cause a mistrial and that–that hoodlum would remain free on bail for another few months."

Miss Duncan pursed her lips and drummed on the desk with her pencil. "I don't quite understand the connection."

Wendy leaned forward earnestly. "If some reporter should write that one of Gallardo's men had tried to kidnap me because of the trial, it might be enough to call for a new trial on the grounds that such a charge could prejudice my father and make it impossible for him to render an impartial verdict."

"I see." Miss Duncan was silent for a long while. "I'll check with the building superintendent and see if he has seen anything or anyone suspicious. I would like to comply with your request, but our first concern must be for the safety of all our girls."

Mr. Olafson came in answer to her call. He was a tall, spare individual with a shining smooth skull where his hair should have been.

"No, I have seen no one around the buildings."

"Think hard. This is a matter of the utmost importance."

"Wait, Miss Duncan. Was this room on the second floor, yes?"

"That is quite right. The girls' rooms are on the second and third floors."

Mr. Olafson grinned sheepishly. "I got to tell you, Miss Duncan," he said, "that new helper of mine. He and I were doing some repair work up there this afternoon, and the man forgot his hammer on the fire escape. A little while ago I see that it is gone, and right away, I send him up to get it."

Miss Duncan sighed her relief.

"I scold him plenty. I give it to him good in the morning. The idea of scaring the girls."

"Perhaps he didn't try to scare us at all," Felicia

put in. "Wendy might have just happened to see him when he came up for the hammer."

"That's right," the Adams girl put in. "He didn't have his face close to the window. Come to think of it now, I'm not at all certain that he was trying to peek in. And yet it seems strange he should stare directly at me."

"But I talk to him. I give it to him. That clumsy, no good dummox." He was still muttering to himself as he went down the hall and the outside steps.

When they were alone, Miss Duncan looked up. "Allow me to congratulate you, Miss Adams," she said. "You have shown good judgment and true Wellington restraint. I should likely have called the authorities and run the risk of creating some highly undesirable publicity had it not been for you."

She rustled the papers on her desk, and the girls rose to go.

Miss Duncan was satisfied with the building superintendent's explanation, but Joan Bailey was suspicious. "What carpenter would leave his hammer?" she asked. "That's like a pilot forgetting where he left his airplane."

"The guy wasn't a carpenter," Felicia reminded her. "He was just the building superintendent's helper."

"Just the same, I'm going to have a look around the first thing in the morning."

"Would you like to move in with us tonight,

Wendy?" the Cartright girl asked. "There's a rolla-way in our closet."

"Certainly not. I'm perfectly safe in my own room."

The following morning Joan was up early and dragged Felicia down to the Adams girl's room.

"Just what do you think you'll find?"

"Maybe nothing. But I don't like the sound of all this. It sounds a little too pat to suit me."

Wendy Adams was uneasy too. She had been up for an hour.

Joan Bailey went to the window, opened it, and looked around.

"Where was the man when you first saw him?" she asked.

"He was out on the fire escape. That's all I know."

"What do you expect to see looking around out there, Joan, another hammer?" Felicia asked, laughing.

The Bailey girl crawled out on the fire escape and began to examine the window casing.

Felicia and Wendy moved close to the window. "What is it?" Wendy asked curiously. "What do you see?"

"Come and see."

They crawled through the window and stared at the lower edge of the window casing and down at the sill. The fresh gouge marks of some sharp instrument were plainly visible.

"It looks as though somebody used some sort of

bar on it," Felicia said, her forehead wrinkling. "You'd almost think he was trying to get the window open."

"Exactly. Does that sound as though whoever was up here yesterday was looking for a hammer?"

Wendy was biting her lower lip.

"We'd better get down and notify Miss Duncan."

When the girls reached the Dean of Women's office, the building superintendent was just leaving.

"You don't have to worry about that man no more, girls," he said. "This morning he didn't even show up for work already. If he comes back now, I fire him, just like that." He snapped his fingers. "He don't come around here and cause trouble. That's for sure."

Miss Duncan listened without comment while Joan told her about the window.

"I'm not at all surprised," she said, "after Mr. Olafson told me that his new man didn't come to work this morning." She picked up the phone. "I'm going to call the police and tell them what happened. They will have a squad car keep an eye on the school for a few nights."

"You won't say anything about me, will you, Miss Duncan?"

"No," the Dean of Women said, "I will not mention you, Miss Adams, unless it becomes necessary."

That evening Miss Duncan granted permission for Wendy to sleep on the rollaway in Felicia's and Joan's room. When the time came to go to bed, Joan read a chapter from the Bible aloud, and she and her roommate knelt to pray. Wendy watched silently but made no comment. They were in bed with the light out before she spoke again.

"I've just made up my mind to something," she said suddenly. "I'm going home this weekend."

"I can't say that I blame you, after what has happened."

"That might have had something to do with it," she said, "but it's not the only reason. I've got to get away. I've got to think."

Felicia was still praying for the girl when she finally drifted off to sleep.

The following morning Wendy went directly from her room to Miss Duncan's office. It was before hours, and the Dean of Women frowned her disapproval. Nevertheless, she listened sympathetically to her request.

"It would probably be all right," she said. "In fact, it might be good for you to spend a couple of days at home now, especially after the events of the last few days. I can well imagine that you are unnerved. But I do not want you to travel alone."

"I'll call my parents. They'll meet me at the train." Miss Duncan picked up the pencil on her desk and tapped it.

"Surely nothing would happen at home," Wendy added.

"Perhaps not. But we feel a certain responsibility for our young ladies. I most assuredly would not want your parents to think that I would take an undue risk with you."

"But I feel that I've *got* to get away for a few days!" she said petulantly.

"Miss Adams, you are wasting your theatricals on me." She spoke coldly. "If you will have Miss Cartright come in and talk with me at her convenience, I'll see if it will be possible for her to accompany you."

Wendy Adams stiffened.

"You mean I've got to take Felicia along?" she demanded sullenly. "Not her!"

Miss Duncan stared at her.

"Miss Adams," she said crisply, "Miss Cartright has been most gracious in her attitude toward you. She is a lovely girl. Considerate, calm, and completely dependable."

"I'm just going home. I scarcely think that I need a chaperone."

"I'm sure that your parents will have the same concern that we have, especially after what happened."

"All right," Wendy agreed when she saw that Miss Duncan was not to be changed. "But can't you send someone else along with me instead of Felicia?"

"I thought you liked Miss Cartright."

Wendy paused. "I do," she said. "In fact, she's my best friend here at school."

"Then why don't you want to take her along?"

"It's that–that fanatical religion of hers," Wendy explained lamely. "I'm going back home where I'll see a lot of my friends. And to put it bluntly, I'm afraid that Felicia would embarrass me."

Miss Duncan leaned forward. Her eyes became eagle sharp. "Miss Adams," she said, "Miss Cartright is a Wellington girl in the best Wellington tradition. She has grace, poise, and a good upbringing. She will not embarrass you or anyone else. I will talk with her. If she will consent to make the trip to your home with you, you have my permission to go."

Wendy's eyes blazed. "That is the only condition on which you'll let me go home?" she demanded.

Miss Duncan's gaze did not waver. "Precisely, Miss Adams," she said. "Precisely."

CHAPTER 5

UNEASY GUESTS

Felicia Cartright agreed to go home with Wendy for the weekend but asked Miss Duncan if Joan might join them.

"I think it will be all right," the Dean of Women said. "Her grades have been considerably better the past few weeks, and I approve rewarding industry."

"You're a doll, Felicia," Joan exclaimed when she heard about it. "A livin', breathin' doll."

"It's not you that we wanted," her roommate said, smiling. "It's that little red convertible of yours."

A pained expression came to Joan's face. "Now you've wounded me. I'll never be able to hold my head high."

"It's not only because I like your company that I asked Miss Duncan if you could go along," Felicia said seriously. "Wendy is beginning to show real interest in Christian things. I thought maybe if you were with us that you might be able to help witness to her."

Joan picked up a file and began to work on her nails. "I had a hard time liking Wendy at first. Even now when she says something deliberately to hurt another person, for a minute I feel as though I want to slap her. But you can't help being sorry for her, can you? She seems to be so miserable."

Felicia nodded.

"It might be that she's always had everything she's ever wanted, but it certainly hasn't made her very happy."

"I'm surprised that she would even let you witness to her."

Felicia picked up her Bible. "I think Wendy sees that the Word of God has the answer to all her problems. That's why this trip is so important. I tell you, Joan, it's an answer to prayer."

* * *

Miss Duncan talked with them for a moment or two before they left for the weekend.

"Did you notify your parents, Miss Adams?" she asked. "Are they expecting you?"

"I notified them. You don't think I'd go all that way and not know whether they're going to be home or not, do you?"

Felicia, who happened to be looking directly at

her, saw a strange look flicker in her eyes. But Miss Duncan seemed satisfied.

They put their suitcases in the car trunk and set out for the turnpike that led up to New Hampshire. Wendy Adams seemed more relaxed than she had been since they had known her. She was almost happy. As Joan drove, Wendy leaned back in the seat and closed her eyes.

"I didn't realize how absolutely bored I was at Wellington," she said, "until now that I'm headed home."

"I wasn't bored at school," Felicia told her, "but I was lonesome and homesick before our first vacation. I could scarcely stand it. After I got home for a day or two, I was anxious to go back."

"I won't be." She sighed deeply. "In fact, I'm not at all sure that I'm going back. I think I'll just stay at home and have fun."

Neither Joan nor Felicia gave any indication that they had heard her.

They stopped briefly at an attractive little cafe, and it was dark when they finally reached Wendy's hometown and pulled up before the big stone house where she and her parents lived.

"The place is dark, Wendy," Joan said. "Are you sure your parents are expecting us?"

"I was afraid old Duncan wouldn't let us come if I told her the truth, and I just had to get away for a couple of days."

"I'm not sure I like this, Wendy," Felicia told her. "You've placed Joan and me in the position of breaking regulations too."

"Now don't act as though I've committed such a terrible crime," she retorted, her voice rising. "Court is in session now, so Dad can't be too far away. The only thing I did was to forget to call and tell them that we were coming."

Joan Bailey got out of the car. "Maybe they've just gone somewhere for the evening," she said. "Besides, we can't spend the night sitting out here. Do you have a key?"

They unlocked the door and went inside. Wendy switched on the light in the living room. The room was as long as many homes, with a vaulted ceiling, period furniture, and a chandelier that must have been created by some long-deceased master glass blower. Felicia and Joan could not avoid staring.

"I thought places like this existed only in fairy stories," Joan Bailey said admiringly. "Wendy, it's magnificent."

"I wish this old dump was in somebody's storybook," Wendy Adams answered, her lips curling about the words. "This is just a big, old barn of a house. I hate it."

"Any time you get tired of it," Joan said, "you can give it to me."

Wendy showed them through the rooms on the

main floor, each as beautiful as the living room, and took them to their rooms on the second floor.

"You can put your things in here," she said to Felicia. "And Joan, you can take the room across the hall. I'm sure these are the rooms Mom would want you to use."

"What time do you think your parents will be home?" Felicia asked uneasily.

Their tall friend shrugged her shoulders. "That's hard to say. Usually the parties they go to on Friday or Saturday nights don't end until late. I think we'd just as well go to bed."

"That," Joan said, "sounds like an excellent suggestion."

They went into the bedrooms Wendy assigned them, but as soon as she was gone, Joan Bailey came slipping into Felicia's room.

"I'm not going to stay in that big room all by myself," she announced, lowering her voice. "There are twin beds here. I'm moving in with you."

"I was just coming into your room." Felicia sat down at the dressing table. "What do you make of all this, Joan?"

"There must be a logical explanation."

"Do you think Wendy knew that her parents weren't going to be home? She didn't act very surprised to see that the house was dark."

"I'd thought of that." She began to put up her hair. "But I don't believe that she did. Her parents are probably out for the evening. When we wake up in the morning, we'll find out all about it."

"Just the same," Felicia continued, "I feel terribly uneasy, and I don't know why."

Joan got her Bible from the suitcase and opened it so they could have their devotions together.

"I wonder if we're going to get a chance to talk with her about the Lord. Did you notice how much on guard she is? If the conversation even begins to drift toward spiritual things, she changes it immediately. She seems determined not to let us witness to her."

"That's just the way I used to be. I liked you a great deal, Felicia, even before I was saved. But I'd get tense and withdrawn every time you headed in my direction. And I didn't rest easily until you were gone. I was afraid of you and against your testimony. You used to scare me."

"But you were open, Joan, even though belligerent. Wendy is secretive."

They had their devotions together, praying for the girl in the other room. They had turned out the light and were just crawling into bed when Felicia heard something downstairs.

She stiffened suddenly and caught her breath.

"Joan."

Her friend sat upright in bed. "Now what's the matter with you? You sound as though you've just seen a ghost."

"I–I haven't seen anything," Felicia said, stammering. "But did you hear that?"

They both listened.

"I can't hear a thing."

"Well, I can."

"It's probably the judge and Mrs. Adams coming home from the party."

Felicia Cartright pursed her lips. "They'd make more noise than that." She reached over to the other bed and found Joan's hand. It was as cold as her own. "Whoever's down there is being as quiet as possible."

"M-maybe they saw my car in the drive and are calling the cops."

The two girls slipped out of bed and tiptoed to the bedroom door. Their room was at the head of the big, open staircase. They opened the door noiselessly and inched out into the hall.

"Joan!" the Cartright girl whispered tensely. "Whoever's down there is in the dark!"

"Do–do you suppose it's Wendy?" she whispered.

"It couldn't be," Felicia countered.

Joan Bailey grasped her companion tightly by the arm. "If it isn't Mr. or Mrs. Adams," she whispered, "and it isn't Wendy, it–it must be someone else!"

"T-t-that's just what I've been thinking!"

CHAPTER 6

REFUGE IN A STORM CELLAR

For a long, agonizing space of time, Felicia Cartright and Joan Bailey crouched at the bedroom door, listening intently. They hardly dared breathe.

Whoever was downstairs was totally unfamiliar with the rooms. He was moving slowly, cautiously. Now and then, he must have bumped into something, for they would hear a dull thud. Then again all was silent.

The girls listened, under strain.

"Do–do you suppose he's gone?" Felicia whispered.

"If he is, he must have floated out," Joan said. "He didn't make any noise going."

"What do you suppose he's doing down there?"

"I–I don't know, and what's more, I don't intend to go down to find out."

For a minute or two, the girls could detect no sound. It almost seemed as though it was all a bad dream. Then the muffled sound of a door being opened, again a piece of furniture being moved, drifted up to them.

"What do you suppose he's doing?" Felicia whispered again.

"Looking for something," her companion answered, shuddering. "And my hope is that he's not looking for us."

"He's not looking for us. He knows that we wouldn't be hiding behind a piece of furniture on the first floor."

"Just the same I don't want to take any chances."

The sounds came closer. The girls caught sight of a faint, yellow beam as it played about the living room.

"A flashlight!" the Bailey girl whispered in desperation.

"And he's coming!"

"What *are* we going to do?" Joan asked, her voice quavering. She grasped Felicia by the arm. "We can't just stand here and wait until he comes up and–and grabs us."

"Let's go waken Wendy," Felicia said, her voice firm. "Let's get a phone. We can call the police."

"How long do you think it will take the police to get here? We haven't got all night, you know? That guy's closing in all the time."

The tall, red-headed Wendy got up quickly when they shook her and slipped into a robe. She was as frightened as Felicia and Joan.

"Is—is there really someone in the house?" she asked incredulously.

"You're not kidding," Joan said excitedly. "In a jiffy, he's going to be up here unless we do something and do it pronto."

Wendy's eyes were wide with fright. "What can we do?"

"We could call the police," Felicia whispered.

"We could," the other girl replied, "but Vendora only has a town marshal. When there is a call at night, there's no way of knowing how long it would take for him to get the message and get over here."

"We don't have time for that," Joan retorted. "We've almost no time for anything. That guy's going to be here shortly. What we do, we've got to do it now."

Felicia thought.

"Is there any place where we could hide?" she asked. "Somewhere that he wouldn't think to look for us."

'There's a closet at the end of the hall," Wendy suggested. "I don't know how good a hiding place that would be. Mom could always find me when I was little and hid there."

"Oh, no," Joan countered quickly. "That guy is going over every room with a fine-tooth comb. He's too thorough. I tell you, he's not going to miss anything, and the chances are that he won't miss anything when he gets up here. He'd be sure to look if we hid in the hall closet."

"But there must be somewhere to hide in a house as big as this," Felicia said.

"I've got it!" Wendy exclaimed, her voice rising a little in excitement.

"Shh-s-shh!" Joan cautioned. "If you aren't careful, we won't even need a place."

"There's a storm cellar with an entrance from the basement," she said. "Built a long time ago, it has a door that can be barricaded from the inside."

"How can we get there?" Joan questioned. "That guy is between us and the basement. I don't think he'd take kindly to it if we'd step out and say, 'Pardon, Sir, but we're on our way to the basement to escape.'"

"There's a back stairway," Wendy said. "Follow me – I'll show you."

She led quickly down the wide hall to a narrow, back staircase. The girls crept along on tiptoes.

"I wish I had my shoes," Joan whispered.

"You can go back for yours if you wish," Felicia told her, "but I'm going to go along with cold feet."

"F-f-forget I said it," Joan said. "When I think about going back, my feet feel warm."

Felicia glanced over her shoulder in time to see a beam of light through a crack flicker onto the hall ceiling. "Hurry! He's coming up the front stairs!"

They made their way to the first floor, across a narrow hallway, and down a second flight of stairs to the basement. Not until they made their way into the storm cellar and securely barricaded the door did Joan speak again.

"This is one trip I should have known better than to take," she said with mock anger. I was well off when I stayed in Wellington. Even studying wouldn't be quite as bad."

"That's one for Miss Duncan," Felicia countered. "I should have a recording of it. She'd feel that her efforts with you were beginning to bear fruit."

Wendy wasn't even listening. She was scurrying around at the back of the storm cellar.

"There ought to be a gas lamp here, somewhere, and matches. Dad always kept them here in case of emergency. He's always been afraid of storms."

"Do you think we ought to have a light?" Felicia asked. "What if this guy comes down the basement? The light shining below the door would be a giveaway."

"This oak door fits tightly. You can't even see if there is a light," Wendy Adams went on. "And even if he did see it, he couldn't possibly get in. This is the safest place in the entire house."

"I don't know about you two," Felicia said, "but I'll feel a great deal better if we have a little light."

"That goes for me, too," Joan added.

In a moment or two, Wendy found the lamp and lighted it. Its white light hurt their eyes momentarily. They blinked and rubbed them.

"I–I just can't understand it," Wendy Adams said

after a time. "I can't understand why anyone would come in and search the entire house in this way."

"It could be a thief who happened to learn that your parents are away," Joan said.

"I don't think so. That kind of thief would be looking for a wall safe or some sort of strong box. He wouldn't go through every room in the house the way this intruder is doing." She shook her head for emphasis. "No, I don't think it's a thief. I can't figure out who it could be or what it is he's after."

Felicia saw by the glare of the light that her face was ashen. Her eyes were wide and staring ahead.

"Wendy," the Cartright girl began severely, "I'm going to ask you some straight questions, and I'm going to expect some straight answers."

Wendy's lips curled in bitterness.

"Now I suppose you think I'm a partner with this individual whoever he is. Can't you give me credit for any honesty?"

"It isn't that at all," Felicia replied. "You didn't seem to be at all surprised when we arrived this evening and found that your mom and dad weren't at home. That's what is perplexing me. Did you know that they weren't going to be here when we left Wellington?"

Wendy Adams straightened haughtily.

"I don't know what sort of a person you think I am," she said angrily. "Do you think I would actually have come here and brought you with me if I thought for a moment that my parents weren't home? Do you really believe I'm that kind of a schemer."

"There are so many things in this that don't add up," Felicia answered. "I just want to be sure. Joan and I have a responsibility you know."

"You can quit worrying or thinking about that right now," Wendy retorted. "I have no intentions whatever of going back to that school."

The belligerent look fled from her face.

"Honestly, Felicia, I thought that Mom and Dad would be here. That's the truth. That's the only reason I wanted to come home this weekend."

"I believe you."

"I don't know what's the matter." Desperation edged Wendy's voice. "There are so many things going on that–that–" She allowed the thought to die away.

Joan, who had been listening at the door, came back to where the girls were standing.

"The other night there was that guy peeking in my room at Wellington. Tonight when we got here, my parents weren't home. And Dad is always home when court is in session, as it is now. Even that's strange. Now there's a prowler probably ransacking the house. I can't help it. I–I'm really frightened!"

CHAPTER 7

A PHONE CALL

*S*ilence enveloped the trio. The girls just stared. Felicia Cartright caught herself listening to their breathing. Her own heart was hammering so loudly she was sure the others must hear it.

Joan started to speak but hesitated and wet her lips nervously.

"Now there's no cause to get so excited we lose our heads and do something foolish," Felicia said. In spite of the heavy beating of her own heart, her voice was calm and even as she spoke.

"There was explanation for the man you saw on the fire escape back at Wellington, you remember. The chances are that there's a logical reason for these other things, too."

"Maybe there's a reason for Mom and Dad being away," Wendy said, "but what about the man in the house?"

"He's obviously just a thief taking advantage of the situation," the Cartright girl answered with a firmness she did not feel. "He probably learned that your parents are gone and seized the opportunity to break in. He knows, or thinks he does, that no one is home, so he's taking his time."

"That could be true," Joan Bailey broke in, "if it weren't for the fact that my car is sitting outside, and the out-of-state license is on it. If he's smart at all, he *knows* that we're probably here."

Wendy was still staring at her companions. Near hysteria was written on her face.

"In all the years that we've lived here," she said, "we've never had anything like this happen." She sighed. "Why would everything begin to happen at once? That's what I want to know." She took Felicia by the arm. "What is going on? What's happening?"

The girls were silent. There was no answer at the moment to Wendy's question.

The three of them huddled together in the storm cellar until morning, pulling their bare feet up under them to keep warm.

"I don't think I'm even going to have any feet," Joan complained, rubbing them gingerly. "I think they're going to freeze off."

"I suggested that you ought to go back and get your shoes."

"You want to get rid of me, don't you?" she

retorted. "You know what would have happened if I'd gone back."

"I wonder if he's still up there?" Wendy asked.

"To tell you the truth, I don't intend to find out." Wendy turned down the lamp and the girls stretched out on the cold floor. Whoever had been or was upstairs did not come near the basement. Toward morning, they dozed off and slept fitfully, but by 7:00 they were wide awake.

Joan awakened first and poked Felicia in the ribs.

"Come on," she said, "time to get up."

The Cartright girl rubbed her eyes. "My feet," she muttered, "they've never been so cold in my life."

"That's what I've been trying to tell you." Joan glanced at her watch. "If that guy is still here, he's more foolish than I think he is."

Wendy sat up next and looked around.

"I had the most horrible dream," she began.

"Don't tell us!" her companions chorused. "That's one thing that we don't want to hear just now."

"But it was about that man."

Felicia turned to Joan.

"Do–do you suppose that it's safe for us to move now?" she asked.

Joan Bailey quietly unbarred the heavy, oak door.

"No burglar would stick around this long," she said. "He'd want to be far away when daylight came."

"Maybe he wasn't a burglar," Wendy repeated for the second time. "Did you ever think of that?"

"If he wasn't a burglar, he'll sure do us until one comes along."

They walked slowly, fearfully, up the basement stairs. Joan was in the lead. Felicia came behind her, and Wendy, who kept glancing back, was in the rear.

"I–I'm almost afraid to open the door," Joan said hesitantly. "What do you say that we turn around and go down to the cellar? I sort of liked it down there."

"I thought your feet were cold."

"T-t-they are. But I still don't think I want to open this door."

"There's nothing to fear but fear," Felicia told her sternly. "Hurry up. We've got to do something."

Joan reached for the door and then drew back.

"H-How do I speak to a b-burglar?" She asked. "Do I say, 'G-G-Good morning?' or do I just scream."

"Knowing you, I'd say that you'd scream."

"You're right."

They entered the kitchen and stood for an instant looking around.

"Did he ever mess things up!" Joan said. "The kitchen looks worse than when you and I make fudge, Felicia."

Wendy pushed past them and went into the dining room. From there they could see into the living room and into the library. Drawers were jerked out of the desks, some overturned. Cushions from the over-stuffed furniture had been slashed.

Wendy led the way to the bedrooms on the first floor.

"Look!" she cried. "They've ruined everything."

Mattresses had been jerked off the beds, dresser drawers were pulled out, their contents were strewn about the floor. Even the wall safe behind a picture in the master bedroom had been found, and it was standing open.

"Do you know what your dad kept there?" Felicia asked.

Wendy shook her head.

"Did he keep money in it?" Joan put in.

"I don't think so," she replied. "If he did, he never mentioned it. Of course, he's always been secretive about things like that."

"If he had any secrets in that safe, they're stolen now," Joan observed, as much to herself as to her companions.

"What are you going to do now, Wendy?" Felicia asked.

"I–I didn't want to call the sheriff," she said uncertainly, "because of publicity, but from the looks of the house, I–I'm afraid that I'll have to. A burglary like this will have to be reported."

Joan and Felicia nodded agreement.

"There must have been a lot of papers," Felicia said, "from the looks of those that are strewn all over the floor."

Wendy decisively called the sheriff's office. A deputy was out in an hour.

Before he arrived, Wendy called another number. "I'm going to call Donna James. She's Dad's private secretary. She'll know where he and Mom have gone."

It was Saturday, and Miss James was still at home.

"Why, Wendy!" she exclaimed. "What are you doing home? Your parents weren't expecting you."

"They weren't home last night!"

"I know that," Miss James said. "They left town yesterday afternoon to be gone for the weekend. They are going to feel terrible when they hear that they've missed you."

Wendy Adams made no attempt to hide her disappointment.

"Do you know where they went?" she asked. "And when they'll be back?"

"No," she answered. "Your dad didn't say where they were going, but I know that they'll be back before Wednesday. The trial was recessed until then."

Miss James was greatly disturbed when she learned that the house had been ransacked. "I'll be right out," she exclaimed.

She and the deputy arrived at the big stone house at about the same time. Mr. Armstrong went from room to room, carefully checking for clues, and asked a few sharp questions.

"We're so close to the city," he said when he had finished, "that we're beginning to have quite a few cases like this. Do you think that anything of value was stolen?"

"I don't think so," Wendy answered, "but I couldn't be sure."

"As soon as the judge returns, we'll get in touch with him and see." He picked up his hat. "Try not to touch anything. The men from the lab are on their way out. They'll want to take photographs and check for fingerprints."

"Do you think there could be any connection between this attempted burglary and the fact that the judge is who he is?" Miss James asked.

"Could be," the officer said, scratching his head, "but I doubt it. It looks routine to me. We see a lot of these cases. Close to the city, you know."

When he was gone, Miss James turned to the girls. "Now the reporters will be out here before long," she said. "You go into the kitchen and get something to eat. Then go to an upstairs room by the back stairs and stay there. With the Gallardo trial under way, this is going to have to be handled very carefully."

The girls went to the kitchen and began to fix breakfast.

"I'm certainly glad that she's here," Joan said. "Did you ever see anyone more efficient? You'd think she handled robberies every day."

"Miss James has been with Dad for twenty years. He always says that he doesn't know what he'd do without her."

When they went upstairs, Wendy went off to her own room for a moment.

"What do you make of all this?" the Bailey girl asked Felicia when they were alone.

"I don't like it at all. I'm afraid that deputy is making a big mistake in assuming that this was an ordinary burglary. It looks to me as though there are plenty of things in this house that are worth stealing. But they weren't touched. Wendy says that she doesn't think a thing was taken."

"I wondered about that too. The way the drawers and the safe were ransacked, it looked to me as though whoever was in here last night was after something else. Papers, maybe."

"And does that guy who peeked into Wendy's window back at school fit in?" Felicia paused thoughtfully. "It might sound melodramatic, but it seems to me that all of these things happening at once is too much of a coincidence to have just happened. There must be a reason."

"But what is it?"

Felicia shook her head. "That's something we will have to find out," she said.

The reporters came about the same time that the technician from the sheriff's office arrived. Miss James answered their questions crisply, permitted them to take a few pictures, and sent them on their way. When they were gone, she called to the girls and had them come downstairs to be fingerprinted.

"This was the work of a professional," the technician said when he had finished comparing their prints with those he found in the house. "There are two other sets of prints here. I presume they belong to the judge and his wife. Outside of them there isn't another fingerprint in the house. And no clues, either. This was a clean job. A mighty, clean job."

"Do you suppose there could have been some other motive besides robbery?" Felicia ventured.

The technician looked up. "The judge is a wealthy man, Miss," he said, "but he's got his enemies because of the job he holds. There could be a great many reasons why Judge Adams' house would be ransacked."

"But the deputy acted as though he thought it was a routine robbery."

"The sheriff doesn't. He's taking charge personally." And then, as though he had already said too much, the technician packed up his gear and left.

"How long are you going to be staying, Wendy?" Miss James asked.

"I think we'll stay until after noon. Then if Mom and Dad aren't back, I suppose we'll have to go back to school." Her inflection left no doubt as to how she felt about it.

"I'm going to the office now. If I hear from your parents, I'll call you at once." She slipped into her coat. "And whatever you do, don't leave town without telling *me*."

The rest of the morning passed slowly. About

eleven o'clock, Joan went out to the supermarket for needed groceries. While she was gone, the home phone rang. Felicia was alone downstairs, so she let the answering machine take the message.

When she heard the caller, she ran and got Wendy.

The caller's voice was garbled and hard to understand, but Wendy's face beamed as she heard the message.

WENDY, WE HAVE COMPLETED
BUSINESS IN BOSTON

AND ARE HEADING FOR OUR SUMMER
HOME

AT MOUNTAIN LAKE. MEET US THERE.

"I've finally heard from Mom and Dad!" Wendy took a deep breath. "You don't know how worried I've been."

"Are you sure it was them? The caller's voice was so hard to understand," Felicia asked.

"Of course, it was them. They're leaving Boston this morning and they want us to meet them at Mountain Lake."

Felicia smiled relief, and then her face clouded with suspicion.

CHAPTER 8

A JOURNEY ENDS IN MYSTERY

When Joan Bailey returned from the store a few minutes later, Wendy had already packed her case and carried it down to the front hall.

"Have you called Miss James?" Felicia asked.

"I'm doing that now."

Joan dropped the sack of groceries on the kitchen table. "What's going on here?" she asked. "Why all the excitement?"

Wendy got through to her dad's secretary and motioned for quiet.

"I was just going to call you," Miss James said.

"Did you hear from Dad too?"

"No, but I had a phone call from the caretaker of the place at Mountain Lake. I called there for the judge this morning after the robbery. He said that he got a message from your mother telling him to open up the house as they would be arriving some-time this evening."

"I don't know what to think about going on to Mountain Lake," Joan said when she learned about the message. "Miss Duncan gave us permission to come here, but she didn't say that it would be all right for us to go anywhere else."

"I can't see what difference that would make," Wendy argued. "We're surely old enough to do what we want to do without asking her permission. All I've heard since I've been there is rules, rules, rules. I almost wish that I'd never heard of the place."

"It isn't that we're not old enough to do what we want to do," Felicia tried to explain. "When we're at school there are certain regulations that we're supposed to keep. One of those is to get permission before we go anywhere."

"Well," Wendy said, pouting, "I don't care what you two do. I'm going up to Mountain Lake to see Mom and Dad."

Felicia thought for a moment.

"I'm sure that it would be all right with Miss Duncan, Joan," she said at last. "She knew that we were coming to see Wendy's parents. She would have given us permission to have gone to Mountain Lake as readily as here. I only hope that the message was from your dad."

"I want to think that."

They finished eating quickly, did the dishes, and

headed up toward Mountain Lake. It was a beautiful, winding drive, and Joan Bailey drove slowly. Every now and then they stopped at a turnout to admire the scene below or to take pictures.

"This is one of the most beautiful places I've ever seen," she said. "You're so fortunate to have a place like this to come to for vacations."

Wendy shrugged indifferently.

"It's all right if you like it," she said. "But as far as I'm concerned, it's old hat. I like to be where there's a lot of excitement. I'd like to spend the summer in a hotel in Boston or New York. That's what I'd like to do."

They had been driving for several hours, and Felicia had said little. Joan spoke to her.

"Now what's the matter with you?" she asked. "You act as though you've lost your best friend."

The Cartright girl shook her head. "I've just been thinking."

"That's one for you," Joan told her. "You'd better stop. It may be catching."

"Wendy," she began suddenly, "has your dad or mom called you at school since you came to Wellington?"

Wendy shook her head.

"I don't think so. No," she went on, "I'm sure of it. They both wrote regularly, but they didn't call." Her lips tightened. "Why?"

"I've been thinking about that."

Felicia was silent for the space of two or three minutes. They passed a sign that said they were sixteen miles from Mountain Lake.

"What made you ask me?" Wendy asked again.

"It just seemed strange to me that he knew where you were," Felicia said. "You said that you didn't tell them that you were coming. How did they learn where you were so they could call you at the house?"

Wendy's face wrinkled thoughtfully. "I just never thought of that."

Joan whistled.

"Perhaps Miss Duncan got in touch with them?" Wendy continued. "You know how disturbed she was."

"She could have," the Bailey girl said. "She makes regular reports. She might have thought it necessary to call today."

"But how would Miss Duncan have learned where they were?" Felicia asked. "Even the judge's private secretary didn't know. And if she had called yesterday, why didn't he wait at home for us or tell his secretary where he was going, so we could have found them?"

"What are you driving at?" Joan asked.

"I'm not sure whether I'm driving at anything," Felicia said. "I've just been asking myself those questions. I haven't been able to come up with any answers that even sound logical."

Joan took an even firmer grip on the wheel.

"We don't really know if it was your dad who called us and left the message."

Wendy Adams massaged her throat. "I am beginning to understand what you're saying," she managed.

"If someone wanted to deceive us into coming up here, that would certainly be a good way."

"Do you suppose someone would do that?" the Adams girl asked.

"If there was a good enough reason," Joan broke in. She turned a corner and shifted into second as they started up the steep grade. Wendy's face paled.

The Bailey girl sighed deeply. "We're right back where we started from. We still don't have the slightest idea whether that message was from your parents or not."

Questions shone in Wendy's eyes – questions and cold, stark fear.

"But you haven't answered me. Why would anyone want to fake a message like that?"

Felicia shook her head.

"I don't know," she answered, "unless someone had good reason to lure us away from the house."

"I don't know why they would want to get us out of the house now," Joan said. "We were there last night, and that didn't stop them."

"Besides, the sheriff knows about it," Wendy put in. "He'll have men in the neighborhood."

"Well," Felicia continued, "the only other reason I can think of is that whoever called, if it wasn't your parents, wanted to lure us up here."

Wendy Adams' cheeks paled. Joan whistled.

"Felicia Cartright," she said sternly, "You can think of the most pleasant things!"

"Perhaps the message was genuine since the caretaker got one too, according to Miss James. Surely no one would go to that trouble to get us up here."

"Unless it was awfully important," Wendy added.

"Well, we'll soon know. We'll probably get up to Mountain Lake and find that Wendy's parents are waiting for us."

"And we'll all have a good laugh," Felicia added.

"That's one laugh that I'll enjoy," Joan muttered. "Believe me."

Joan pressed on the accelerator, and the car moved quickly along the mountain road.

"I'm heading this way against my better judgment, Felicia," she said. "I hope you realize that."

They all laughed nervously.

The sun was almost down when they pulled into the driveway of the Adams' summer home on Mountain Lake. It was a big, rambling frame house with a massive stone fireplace and an immaculate lawn. Nicer than the homes most people lived in the year round.

"Well," Felicia said to no one in particular, "we made it."

"It doesn't look as though Wendy's parents are here. There's no car in sight."

"They often charter a float plane and fly up," Wendy explained, "especially if they're in a hurry.

But I don't believe that they're here yet, or they'd be out to greet us."

"Somebody's been here," Joan said getting out. "The shutters have been opened and the shades are up."

"The caretaker got a message too. Remember?"

For two or three minutes the girls stood beside the car, looking about uneasily.

"Well," Wendy asked at last, "what are we going to do?"

"We went into one empty house," Joan said cryptically. "I can tell you I'm certainly not hankering to go into another."

Felicia laughed at her.

"I'm sure my parents will be here before long," Wendy Adams said. "Dad would never have left that message if he hadn't planned on being here – that is, if he left it."

"They could have been delayed," Felicia answered.

The girls had been moving toward the house but were still on the front steps when a float plane came winging overhead. They stopped and stared up at it.

"I believe it's going to land," Wendy said excitedly. She set down her suitcase and ran around the corner of the house. "That could be Mom and Dad!"

The plane banked sharply and began to circle, losing altitude.

"It's them," she said tensely. "I just know it is."

Felicia and Joan watched silently.

The plane straightened out and began to nose toward the lake.

"He's heading in a peculiar direction if he's coming here," Joan remarked.

An instant later the floats touched down, and the plane began to slow. Instead of turning, however, it continued up the lake.

Wendy Adams sighed in disappointment. "I was so sure that was Mom and Dad," she said. She turned to her companions. "What do you suppose we ought to do?"

"Actually," Felicia answered, "this doesn't change things at all. That message said they were coming. They'll surely be here."

Joan Bailey was the first to start again. "If we're going to stay," she announced, "we'd just as well go inside and stay. There's no point in standing here."

They went into the living room, and Wendy threw herself into an easy chair. "This is one time that I'm going to be glad to see my parents," she said. "This has been one of the worst days I've put in. It's been a terrible day. A positively, terrible day!"

"I don't know that I'd go so far as to say that," Joan said, "but I've got to agree – it's had its moments."

"When did that message say your parents would be here?" Felicia asked.

Wendy frowned.

"I thought it said that they'd be here tonight, but now that you mention it, I'm not sure. No, I don't think it did. All it said was that they were coming up and for us to meet them here."

"It seems strange, though, that they haven't arrived."

"I'm not so sure," Wendy continued. "That letter I got from Mom said that Dad was so concerned about this case that she didn't want me to bother him. Their delay could have something to do with that." -

"I suppose you could be right," Joan said. "But just the same, I think we ought to go down the mountain and stay at a hotel. I'd feel much safer there."

For a moment, Wendy stared at her. Then she laughed nervously.

"You, afraid, Joan? I'm surprised at you. What's the matter with your Christian faith? Or don't you dare trust it too far?"

Joan shrugged. "I guess I can take it if you can."

The girls showered and changed into other clothes. By this time, darkness began to settle. Wendy said nothing but kept going to the window and staring down the mountain road apprehensively.

Felicia Cartright got out her Bible and began to thumb the pages. "We're all a little jumpy and upset tonight," she said. "I think it would be nice if we had our devotions together."

Wendy muttered. However, as Felicia began to read, she came over and sat down across from her, then listened intently. When the time came for prayer, she closed her eyes and bowed her head.

CHAPTER 9

A MORNING AT CHURCH

The evening dragged its shuffling feet. Felicia and her companions made an effort to read but spent most of the time staring around the room or watching the road. Eleven o'clock came and went, and still Judge and Mrs. Adams had not arrived.

"Wendy," Felicia said, getting to her feet and trying to sound calm and unconcerned, "I'm sure that your parents won't be coming now. I think we had just as well turn in. They'll probably be here tomorrow."

"Let's listen to the news first," Joan said. She crossed the room and switched on the TV.

"Judge Adams could not be reached for comment today in the controversial Rocky Gallardo racketeering trial," the announcer was saying. "The judge granted a recess until Wednesday morning to study a defense motion to dismiss the charges against Gallardo for lack of evidence–"

"Hear that?" Joan asked. "That's probably the reason your parents haven't arrived. Your dad is working. They're probably in some out-of-the-way hotel room where he won't be bothered."

"That's what I've been trying to tell myself," Wendy went on. "I know that this trial has been of tremendous concern to him."

They were still talking in hushed tones when the phone rang. They all jumped.

"W-w-what was that?" Joan stammered.

"The phone, silly. Answer it."

It rang again.

"It's probably Mom and Dad." Wendy answered the phone.

"Is this Judge Adams' home?" a masculine voice asked brusquely.

"It–it is. But he isn't here."

"Can you tell me where I might be able to reach him? It's urgent."

Wendy's face was a mask. "Who is this, please?"

"I'm Tom Morgan. Special feature writer for the *Boston Tribune*."

"I'm very sorry, but Judge Adams is not here."

"But he is expected?"

"Sooner or later."

"And who are you?" He shot the question out quickly.

"I'm Wendy Adams." When she hung up, she turned back to her companions. "It was a reporter.

He ought to know that it won't do any good for him to talk with Dad. He will never make comment on a case he's hearing until after it's concluded."

Felicia started to speak but stopped abruptly.

Wendy moved toward her bedroom. "I don't know what you two are going to do, but I'm turning in."

"Sounds like a good idea. Come on, Felicia. Or do you want to sit up all night?"

When they were in their rooms together, the Cartright girl said, "Do you suppose that phone call was actually from a reporter?"

Joan turned. "Felicia," she said, "I have been wondering about that too. It's enough to make a person jumpy."

"It is unreal. But I've had the strangest feeling all day. And just now when I heard that announcer tell about Rocky Gallardo, cold chills ran up and down my spine. That man is desperate, Joan. He'd do anything."

"Yes, but we are far enough away from him so he can't hurt us. In fact, we don't even know him."

Felicia laughed uneasily.

"I guess you're right. Skip it."

Joan Bailey shuddered. "Skip it; you say. After giving me enough to worry about to turn my raven locks white, I suppose in a minute you'll be saying, 'Now go to sleep, honey, and have nice dreams.'"

"I think I'll go and check the locks on the doors

first," Felicia said, slipping into her robe and starting for the living room.

"Check the windows while you're at it," Joan called after her. "I'll go and close the draft on the fireplace. We can't take any chances."

Felicia Cartright went first to the front door, and then to the back. She was thankful that they were both provided with chain guards as well as heavy cylinder-type locks. The windows were locked too. She felt a little silly checking them and yet–.

"Well," she said to Joan when she returned to their room and crawled into bed, "everything's locked up tight. You're as safe as a baby in a crib."

"That's debatable."

"Good night."

In the soft moonlight she could see Joan, in the bed across the room, cup her hands behind her head.

"Know something, Felicia," she said, "the next time some sweet, innocent, little underclassman inveigles me into going along home with her to chauffeur and chaperone her, you'll know it. I'll say, 'No, thank you. I'm afraid that my blood pressure just couldn't stand such a weekend.'"

"You know that you wouldn't miss any of this for the world," Felicia said, laughing.

Joan raised on an elbow and stared at her.

"Just try me, Felicia Cartright. Just try me. I'll tell you this much, it's not exactly my idea of fun to have mysterious messages and phone calls and men prowling around the house in the middle of the night."

"Stop it!" her roommate said, shuddering. "Now you're getting me edgy."

"I thought you were the brave one."

"Not me. I'm afraid of my shadow."

There was a moment's silence. "I'm not scared," Joan said. "I'm not scared at all. But I can tell you this much: if I had a gun, I'd be sleeping with it under my pillow."

They had just turned out the light when Wendy Adams came tiptoeing into their bedroom.

"Joan. Felicia," she whispered. "Are you asleep?"

Instantly they both sat up, staring into the darkness.

"Now what's the matter?" the Bailey girl demanded hoarsely.

"Did–did you hear something?"

"That was just my teeth chattering," Joan told her. "Or maybe it was my heart hammering against my ribs. They're both working overtime."

Felicia sat on the side of her bed.

"Is something wrong?"

"No," she said slowly, "I don't think so, but I can't get to sleep. I'm afraid to be in my room alone."

"Come in here with us," Felicia prompted.

"May I? I'll pull the rollaway in."

Joan got out of bed. "I'll help you."

A minute or two later, they were again settled.

"If anybody is going to come messing around

tonight," Joan said, "I hope they do it before I get to sleep. I don't want to be awakened."

Felicia didn't think that she would be able to sleep at all that night. But she had not realized how tired she was until she got into bed. She closed her eyes momentarily, and the next thing she knew, it was morning. The sun was riding high above the mountains.

She looked over at Wendy and Joan. In spite of their protestations, they, too, had slept soundly. Joan was curled in the covers with her head buried in the pillow. Felicia got up and jerked the covers off her roommate.

"Come on, Joan. Time to get up."

She only grunted.

"Out of bed. We've got to get breakfast and get to church. Get up."

The girls sat up sleepily, rubbing their eyes.

"Know what?" Joan said brightly. "We made it after all."

"Made what?"

"We did live through the night."

"Oh, you!" Wendy made a face at her.

They dressed and went to check the doors.

"They're still locked," Felicia said.

"And," Joan added, "what's more, we didn't even have anyone slip up and try them."

"How do you know that?" Wendy asked.

"Elementary, my dear Miss Adams," Joan said.

"Elementary. I simply sprinkled a little flour on the step before each door. There are no footprints."

"You're amazing," Felicia told her. "I don't know how we'd get along without you."

"That's not worrying me at the moment," Joan said. "Right now, my chief concern is, do we hold out until Judge and Mrs. Adams get here, or do we head back to Wellington? I didn't think I'd ever live to see the day when I'd be so glad to get back there."

Felicia smiled.

"You try to make us think that you're just living until the day you graduate," she said. "But you know that you love the school as much as the rest of us."

"Maybe Joan does," Wendy said curtly, "but I'm quite sure that I could get along without it."

Wendy Adams did not want to go to church that Sunday morning.

"I'm afraid that my parents will come or call," she said lamely.

"We'll only be gone for an hour and a half," Felicia said hopefully. "We can leave a note."

"What if they call the house?"

"They'll surely call again."

"I don't see why going to church is so important," Wendy said. "Or why you keep after me all the time."

"Going to church isn't going to get you to heaven," Felicia explained. "Only by confessing your sin and trusting in the Lord Jesus can you become a Christian."

"There you go again." She whirled and flounced out of the room.

Felicia and Joan got ready for church and started for the car. To their surprise, Wendy joined them.

"I changed my mind," she said brightly. "I'm sure that my parents won't be here before we get back."

The church was small, and only half the pews were filled, but the message was sharp and straightforward. The minister told the simple, salvation story. It was driving to the very depths of Wendy's heart. Felicia was sure of that. Every now and then she cast a quick glance at her. As far as Wendy Adams was concerned, there was not another person in the little church auditorium. She leaned forward ever so slightly, her gaze fastened on the speaker.

"*The wages of sin is death,*" the pastor read from the Bible, "*but the gift of God is eternal life through Jesus Christ our Lord.*"

Felicia saw Joan's eyes lower. She knew that her roommate was praying that God would convict Wendy of sin and make her see her need for a Savior. She did not move during the invitation and was still sitting motionless when the benediction was given and others began to leave.

"Wendy," Felicia said softly.

For the moment, Wendy did not move.

"Wendy."

"Wendy."

She lifted her head. Her eyes were blazing.

"Now don't start preaching at me again!" she

snapped. In her anger, she did not realize that they were still in church, and her voice was surprisingly loud. Several turned quickly to look at her. She flushed scarlet, got to her feet, and went hurrying blindly out the door.

Joan and Felicia stared after her, then followed.

"The poor girl," a kind, old lady said to them. "I will be praying for her."

They went to the car and got in. Wendy sat in the back, primly, staring straight ahead. Joan got in the car but made no move to start the engine. Felicia closed the door on her side.

"Well," Wendy Adams lashed out at last, "are we going back to the house, or are we going to sit here all day?"

Felicia turned to her momentarily.

"Wendy," she began, her voice gentle, but insistent, "wouldn't you like to put your trust in the Savior right this minute?"

"Leave me alone!" Wendy cried. "I've had all the preaching that I can stand. Leave me alone!"

"But we haven't been preaching," the Cartright girl continued. "The Holy Spirit must be talking to you, telling you that you need to put your trust in Jesus."

Joan started the car. Wendy drew her mouth into a thin line and looked at neither Joan nor Felicia until they got back to the Adams' summer home. When they reached the house, she said icily, "Whatever you do, don't ask me to go to that miserable, little church tonight. It was the most boring morning. I couldn't bear to sit through it again."

With that, she turned and stomped off toward the house alone.

"If there was just some way that we could reach her." Joan said sorrowfully. "It's hard when people try to fight against God."

For some reason, Wendy Adams went directly to her dad's study. As Felicia and Joan reached the front door, they heard Wendy scream.

"Wendy!" the other two cried, running to her. "What's the matter? What's wrong?"

"S-s-s-somebody's been here," she said weakly, her voice shaking. "Look!"

Indeed, somebody had been in the study. The room had been neat before they left for church. Felicia and Joan had both been in it. Now papers from the huge mahogany desk were strewn across the top and on the floor. Drawers had been pulled out and overturned.

"Something terrible is going on," Joan gasped.

Felicia felt the color leave her cheeks. She reached for Joan's hand. It was cold and moist. They were still standing, staring around the little room, when the phone rang suddenly.

They all jumped!

"What was that?" Felicia cried.

It rang again!

CHAPTER 10

DIRECTION AND
PURPOSE IN LIFE

Wendy Adams crossed to the desk and answered the phone.

"Oh, Dad!" she exclaimed. "Dad!"

"What are you doing up there, Wendy?" he asked. "Why aren't you at Wellington?"

"I–I wanted to talk with you and Mom about something very important," she began, "so I got permission from Miss Duncan to bring two friends home for the weekend. But you weren't there."

"You didn't let us know your plans."

"But I thought sure you would be there, and then when I got your message, I expected you and Mom to be up here last night. When you didn't come, I've been almost frantic with worry."

"Message?" he repeated. "I didn't leave a message. What's this all about?"

He spoke loudly so that both Joan and Felicia could hear him.

"I called Miss James just now," he continued. "She told me about the message you were supposed to have received from Mom and me."

"That's right. And Mr. Anderson got one too. He had the house opened and cleaned when we got here."

"That's strange. That's very strange. We didn't even have any plans for the summer place, and we most certainly didn't send a message."

"That's not all," Wendy blurted. "When we got back from church just now, we found that somebody had broken into the house and rifled your study."

"What?"

"The drawers are out of the desk, and there are papers scattered all over the place."

"That's outrageous!" he exclaimed. "Miss James has told me about the break-in at home, now this."

"Should I call the authorities?" she asked.

He was silent for a moment. "I don't believe that would be wise, at least for the present." He spoke crisply. "I'll tell you, Wendy. Pull the blinds in the study and make sure the windows are securely locked. Then go out and lock the door. And whatever you do, don't touch anything. I'll stop for the sheriff as I come through the county seat."

Wendy sighed her relief.

"I'll be so glad when you get here!"

"We've got quite a trip, my dear," he said, "so it may be fairly late, but we'll make it as soon as we can."

When she finally stopped talking, Joan and Felicia were standing, one on either side.

Wendy Adams was pale and quite breathless.

"You were right about one thing, Felicia," she said. "Dad didn't leave that message, and he didn't send one to Mr. Anderson."

"That tells us one thing," Joan said. "Whoever did knew enough about the family to know your name and where you were at school."

"And he knew the name of the caretaker at your summer home," Felicia put in.

Wendy Adams walked to the door and back uneasily. "I still can't figure it out. If anyone wanted to break into the house here, why didn't they go ahead and do it? Why did they lure us up here?"

"While you're asking questions," Felicia said, "why did that guy peek into your window out at school? What was he looking for? Is there any connection between that and what has been happening since? And what was that guy doing in your house last night? How about that reporter's call? There are a host of questions that just aren't answered."

"There's one more that bothers me," Joan Bailey said, shivering. "What's going to happen next?"

The girls checked the windows in Mr. Adams' study as he had directed and securely locked the door.

"Now," Wendy said, "that's done."

"Where were your parents?" Felicia asked. "And when will they be here?"

Wendy shook her head.

"He didn't say," she answered. "I was so excited that I forgot to ask. But they must have been quite a distance away. Dad said that it would be dark before they got here."

They sat down in the living room and looked at one another silently.

"You know," Joan said after a time, "we're not being very practical today."

"I thought we were being very practical," Felicia replied.

"Well, we're not. Here it is 1:30, and we haven't even started dinner."

"You can't be very frightened." Felicia got to her feet and started for the kitchen. "You're still thinking of food."

Wendy followed. Her face was sallow, and her eyes were dull and fearful.

"I don't think that I could eat a thing." She sighed and glanced at her watch.

They fixed some cold meat sandwiches and found a couple of cans of vegetables and a can of fruit in the cupboard.

"The first one who makes a crack about the food gets the privilege of getting supper tonight," Joan informed them.

All weekend, Felicia and Joan had been taking

turns asking the blessing before their meals. Wendy had always waited and bowed her head respectfully. However, on this occasion, she took a sandwich from the plate almost as soon as she sat down.

"Joan," Felicia said, "would you ask the blessing, please?"

Wendy muttered.

"I suppose you think you've got a better chance to work on me because I'm frightened." She took a small bite from her sandwich, almost defiantly. "You're really going to put pressure on me to go for that religion of yours, aren't you?"

"No," Felicia told her simply, "we wouldn't try to scare you, or anyone else, into accepting Christ. You'll have to come to Him because you realize you need salvation. You've got to come to Christ desiring to put your whole trust in Him."

Felicia and Joan tried hard to talk with Wendy about other things throughout the afternoon. She kept coming back again and again to the subject of Christianity, or religion, as she called it. Now she would ask a question seriously, in all earnestness. A moment later she would lash out in derision.

"Just what has following Christ done for either of you?" she asked. "Name something."

"For one thing," Joan said, "it's given me some control over that miserable temper of mine. And for another, it's given me the assurance of salvation."

"Being a Christian has helped me so much," Felicia

said, "that I wouldn't know where to begin. For one thing, it has given direction and purpose to my life. And happiness. I don't see how anyone could be happy, even for a day, without the Savior."

Wendy Adams looked at her wistfully.

"I don't think I'd have the courage to live a Christian life. I don't think that I could do it, even if I wanted to do it.

"That's where the Lord Jesus comes in," the Cartright girl continued. "None of us can live a good Christian life in his own strength. But if we put our trust in Jesus, looking to Him for the strength to live the way we should, then our lives can really count for Him."

Wendy turned, without comment, and went to her room.

CHAPTER 11

NOW WHERE IS WENDY?

Wendy Adams went into her room and didn't come out for the rest of the afternoon.

"Do you think she's all right?" Joan whispered.

"She was when she went in," Felicia said.

"The poor girl. I know just how she feels. I was the same way for weeks before I accepted the Lord. I wish there were something we could do."

"So do I." The Cartright girl laid aside her magazine. "We've done all we can. This decision is one that she must make herself, either to accept Christ as her Savior or to reject Him."

"If she could only know how wonderful it is to be a Christian."

Felicia sauntered to the picture window overlooking the lake and the mountain behind it.

"Joan, did you ever see anything so beautiful?"

Her roommate walked over, and they stood, arms locked, looking out over the placid water.

"I see that our friends with the float plane are still around," Joan said, pointing to the place where the plane was tied.

"I thought perhaps Wendy's parents would fly up here when they learned what happened."

The Bailey girl looked at her watch. "They should be getting here any time. They couldn't have been that far away."

Darkness seemed to come earlier up in the mountains. One minute, the sun was shining; the next, the light paled, and the shadows ran together. Wendy Adams came out of her room and stared out across the tree-covered slope. She clasped her arms and shivered.

"I can't understand what's keeping Mom and Dad," she said. "You don't suppose they've had some sort of trouble, do you?"

"Didn't he say that it might be after dark before they got here?" Joan asked.

She turned back to them. "I guess so. But I'm getting nervous. I'll be glad when they do get here!"

They ate their evening meal and washed the dishes. They were just finishing when Joan glanced at her watch.

"If we're going to get to church on time, we're going to have to hurry."

Felicia went into the bedroom to dress.

"Do you *have* to go to church tonight?" Wendy demanded of Joan. Her lips curled bitterly about the words.

"No," the Bailey girl answered, "we don't have to go. Is there some reason why we shouldn't? I mean if you're afraid to stay alone or something."

"Why don't you go with us?" Felicia called from the bedroom. "I'm sure the service won't last more than an hour. Your parents ought to be home by the time we get back."

"Oh, no," Wendy said firmly. "No, thanks, I'm not going to waste my time going to hear that–that rabble rouser again. Even if I liked what he said, I wouldn't go back after the way he insulted me this morning."

"We'll be back as soon as we can."

Felicia paused at the door. "Are you sure that you'll be all right?"

"Now you sound like Miss Duncan. Of course, I'll be all right. I'm quite capable of taking care of myself. Go ahead and go to church if you feel that you can't get along without it. Don't mind me."

"I almost wish that we weren't going to church tonight," the Cartright girl said uneasily as she and Joan got into the car and backed out of the driveway. "I feel terribly uneasy about leaving her alone."

"I don't think that she wanted us to go either," Joan replied, "but she was too proud to let us know it."

Felicia laid her hand on her friend's arm. "Do you suppose that we ought to go back?"

"No," Joan said. "That would make her all the angrier."

As they drove along, Felicia became more anxious about leaving Wendy.

"You know, Joan, I think we ought to turn back. I don't think we should have left Wendy alone."

"I think you're right," Joan replied as she slowed the car for a U-turn.

"Well," Felicia said as they drove into the yard once more, "the Judge and Mrs. Adams aren't here yet. At least their car isn't in sight."

"Wendy will be awfully glad to see us. And I know that I feel a lot better now that we're home."

Joan slipped the key out of her red convertible, and they walked across the close-cropped grass together. The lights were on in the living room and one of the bedrooms.

"I wonder where she is," Joan said. "I thought she'd come flying out as soon as we drove up."

"She must be angry."

On the porch, the Bailey girl grasped Felicia by the arm. "Look! The front door is open!"

"And look at the chair in the living room – it's overturned!"

"Wendy!" Felicia cried, running through the house. "Wendy! Where are you?"

There was no answer.

Joan dashed into the kitchen and utility room while her roommate made for the bedrooms.

"Wendy! Wendy!"

A moment later, they were back in the living room staring at one another, horror written on their faces.

"She's not here. She's gone," Felicia said numbly. "She's gone."

"There's been a fight in this front room. Just look at it!"

The living room was a shambles. Furniture had been overturned, and one of the drapes had been jerked from the window.

"W-w-what do you suppose happened?" Felicia's lips scarcely formed the words.

For a long, miserable time, they stared at one another bleakly.

"They've carried her away! She's been kidnapped!"

It scarcely seemed possible in so short a time. And yet Wendy was gone. An end table was knocked over, and a floor lamp had been broken – mute evidence that she had been taken against her will.

"I just can't believe it." Felicia moved woodenly across the floor to the overturned chair. There on the floor, half under a cushion, was a newspaper. She stooped, almost mechanically, and picked it up.

GALLARDO TRIAL RECESSED! The headlines screamed.

"What's that?" Joan cried.

Pinned to the paper with a stiletto-type letter opener was a large, white envelope.

"W-w-what is it?" Joan asked again.

"It's for Judge Adams! His name's on it!"

"Now where do you suppose that came from?"

But Felicia did not answer her. She removed the envelope from the paper and held it momentarily. It was addressed to the judge.

"Do you suppose it gives a clue as to what happened to Wendy?"

The envelope was not sealed. "I wonder what's in it? Should we open it?"

"If it's not sealed and this is an emergency, why not?" Joan Bailey took the envelope from her decisively and removed a single sheet of note paper.

They both gasped when they read it. Someone had used an old typewriter and wrote in bold capitals:

JUDGE! IF YOU WANT TO SEE YOUR

DAUGHTER ALIVE YOU KNOW WHAT
TO DO TO GALLARDO!

"That's why they took Wendy!" Felicia said.

"Those men are desperate. They want to force the judge to let this Gallardo go free."

"And what if Judge Adams doesn't set Gallardo free? What will happen?" Felicia shuddered, and cold sweat broke out on her forehead.

"He can't set Gallardo free on Wendy's account," Joan said. "No honorable judge would. But we can't just stand here until the judge comes. We've got to do something!"

"I'm going to call the authorities!" She dashed to the study, unlocked the door, and fumbled for the phone.

Joan followed close behind, switching on the light.

For the space of a heartbeat, Felicia froze at the phone. She looked at it frantically.

"What is it?" Joan cried. "Why don't you call?"

"Something's wrong. The phone is dead."

"They've cut the line!" Joan exclaimed.

Felicia dropped the receiver. "Our phones won't work out here. Now what?"

"They're not going to stop us easily. Come on. We'll drive down to the village and call the sheriff from there!"

"Hurry!" Felicia said as they ran across the lawn to the car. "There's not a moment to lose! We've got to find Wendy before they take her too far away!"

They jumped into the car and Joan tried to start the car, but the engine wouldn't turn over.

"Felicia!" Joan exclaimed. Those guys who kidnapped Wendy must have fixed the car so it wouldn't run!" She reached over and switched off the ignition. "We must have gotten here minutes after they took Wendy, or they wouldn't have been around to sabotage the car."

"Or," the Cartright girl added, "someone could have been hiding here waiting for us."

Joan cringed. "Just the thought gives me goose bumps."

"We've got to get help, Joan. But the telephone line is cut, and they've fixed the car. Now what do we do?"

CHAPTER 12

THE TAKE-OFF

Joan Bailey bowed her head and began to pray. Felicia did the same. Moments later they raised their eyes.

"It's more than five miles to the village," Joan said firmly. "It would take too long to walk there."

"There's no knowing where Wendy would be by that time."

"If her parents would only come! They'd know what to do!"

"But there's no telling when they'll get here either." Felicia's voice was tinged with desperation. "What should we do, Joan?"

"Aren't any of the summer houses around the lake open? Surely one would have a phone."

"But it's too late in the season for summer visitors. And the people who come up Friday night for the weekend have already gone back."

Joan walked speculatively around the corner of the house and glanced around the lake. There were no lights visible.

"There's the float plane!" she exclaimed. It's still here. Someone there can help us!"

"I'll go in and write a note to Wendy's parents," Felicia said. "It'll only take a minute."

She scribbled a note to Judge Adams and quickly pinned it on the overturned chair where he could not miss seeing it.

Together she and Joan started up the road toward the place where the float plane was docked.

"I wonder about the kidnappers" Joan said. She glanced about apprehensively.

"What gave you the pleasant thought that they still might be hanging around?"

"One of them was here when we drove in, remember?" she asked. "He hung around long enough to fix our car."

"We can't worry now. I keep thinking that every minute we take might make the difference in whether we get Wendy or not."

"This whole thing seems like an ugly dream," her companion replied.

At last, they reached the place where the float plane was tied.

"Oh, Joan!" Felicia cried in dismay, "there's no one here! The house is dark!"

The summer cottage looked deserted. There were no lights on in the side facing them.

"Are you sure we've come to the right place?"

"Isn't that the plane?" From where they stood, they could see only dimly the hulk of a large object at the water's edge. As they drew nearer, they could see that it was a plane.

"This is the place, all right," Felicia whispered, "but I don't think anyone's home."

"There's got to be." Joan strode boldly up on the porch. "Look, Felicia! The front door is open!"

The front door was ajar, and the screen door was hooked from the inside.

"There must be someone here."

"There is!" Felicia said excitedly. "I can hear talking!"

Joan reached over and touched the bell. It rang suddenly, raucously. Although they were both expecting it, the sound of it startled them. They waited. The muffled tone of voices from inside the cottage ceased. No one came to the door.

"Ring it again," the Cartright girl said softly.

Joan pressed on the bell once more.

There was a muffled curse from deep inside the house. "Pete," the voice said. "There's somebody at the door!"

"Shut up, Harry!" The last voice was hoarse, almost a whisper.

"Hurry, please!" Joan shouted impetuously "We've got to use your phone! It's a matter of life or death!"

"Those girls!" the one called Pete cursed again, savagely. "I told you we should have taken care of them. I told you!"

"Joan!" a familiar voice screamed. "Joan! Felicia! Run!"

"Shut up!" Pete ordered. "I told you if you behaved yourself you wouldn't get hurt! But we're not going to stand for any foolishness! Now sit down and shut up!"

The girls did not wait to hear more. Somebody was dashing madly for the front door!

"This way," Felicia cried. She jumped off the porch and into the brush. Joan was right behind her.

"Don't worry, boss!" Pete shouted. "I'll get 'em! And when I do, they'll be mighty sorry they ever came messing around."

"Come on, Pete," his companion ordered firmly, "there isn't time to fool around with them! We've got to get out of here!"

"But, boss!"

"By the time they can get any help, we'll be long gone. Tear that phone out and bring the girl. I'll go out and warm up the plane!"

Felicia and Joan lay in the brush fifty or sixty yards away, panting heavily.

"Felicia," Joan whispered in agony, "they're going to fly Wendy away!"

"I didn't think they could take off from the water at night."

"Sure, if they've got lights on the plane. It wouldn't be different from taking off from the ground."

Felicia thought for a moment. "Come on, we've got to do something!"

Joan followed as she crept stealthily through the trees to the water's edge. In the inky blackness, they could just make out the faint outline of the plane. It was a little larger than the average small plane.

"I don't know whether my scheme will work or not, but we've got to try." Felicia glanced quickly around. "Every summer cabin on a lake has a boat. Do you see one here?"

"Tied out to the dock," Joan answered.

The people who owned the place must not have done much boating, for the only boat they had was an old, flat-bottom scow.

"Come on," Felicia said. "That ought to do."

They moved quietly out to the end of the dock and got into the boat.

"Help me get the boat untied and over next to the plane," Felicia Cartright whispered. "We'll tie the anchor rope to one of the pontoons. With a drag as heavy as the boat, they won't be able to take off."

"That's right."

Joan had just finished untying the scow when the pilot came out and started the engine. The roar of the motor shattered the hush of the night.

"We've got to hurry. They'll be taking off in a minute."

Neither girl was prepared for what happened next. Before they were able to put the oars into the locks, the pilot switched on the plane's powerful headlights and began to move it slowly out to the dock. The beam swept over them, inches above their heads, as the plane came around. They pressed against the bottom of the boat.

CHAPTER 13

A COLD NIGHT TO SWIM!

As the plane began to inch along the dock, the cottage door opened, and two figures came out. One had the girl by the arm and was half dragging her along. Crouching in the bottom of the boat, Felicia and Joan could not see what was going on, but they heard the man curse loudly.

"Now get along with you!" he snapped. "And no funny business!"

"You don't have to hold my arm so tight," Wendy complained. "I'm not going to run."

"I'll say you're not! We're going to make good and sure of that! You're Rocky Gallardo's insurance."

"My dad will never let a thing like this influence him," she retorted. "He's an honest judge."

"That's why we grabbed you, sister. We want to be sure that he stays honest and lets Rocky go free."

"He'll never do it."

"You'd better hope that he does." He cursed once more. "You'd just better hope that he does!"

The man in the plane opened the door and called, "Hurry it up, Pete. We haven't got all day."

"All right, sister! Get into that airplane!"

Wendy Adams passed so close to Joan and Felicia that either of them could have reached out and touched her. Yet they didn't dare move or talk.

A moment later Wendy Adams and the two men were in the plane. The door closed, and the pilot eased the throttle forward. There was a deepening throb to the motor as the plane glided away from the dock. The light ahead was so brilliant that it made the darkness seem all the more intense.

"Hard on the oars, Joan!" Felicia shouted. "Get me over to the tail!"

They were almost behind the plane now and the blast from the propeller drove through their clothes.

Joan did as she was told, and the heavy boat moved forward sluggishly.

Fortunately, the engine wasn't yet warm enough for the take-off, and the man at the controls held the plane to a crawl with the flaps.

Felicia snatched up the anchor and crouched tensely in the prow. There was only a chance! Prayerfully she waited until the boat almost bumped the tail section of the plane.

It all happened as smoothly as though timed with a metronome. The boat surged forward as Joan pulled hard on the oars. Felicia straightened, tossed the light anchor over the fuselage, and ducked as the tail section glided over them.

"Felicia!" Joan exclaimed, horrified. "We'll both be killed!"

Almost at that very moment, the pilot decided that all was in readiness. The throb of the motor became a roar. The light float plane leaped forward.

"Hang on!"

The plane reached the end of the unusually long anchor rope. There was a sudden lurch. Felicia and Joan were almost thrown from the boat.

"W-w-what do we do now?" the Bailey girl demanded.

In the same instant, the plane motor was cut off. The silence was deafening.

"What did we hit, boss?" Pete asked hoarsely. "What was that?"

"Look out and see if there's a dead head in the water. We hit something, and it felt like an old log."

Pete took the flashlight and climbed down to the float. Felicia and Joan crouched down in the bottom of the boat, waiting fearfully and praying.

"Everything seems to be all right."

"How are the floats?"

"Okay, I tell you." He flashed the light, speculatively, in a wide arc. "Are you sure there isn't anything wrong with the plane?"

"There couldn't be. I checked it myself this afternoon."

He paused, and Pete started to climb back into the little cabin. "Are you sure those floats aren't damaged?"

"Positive. Check them yourself."

"Just wanted to make sure. Get in! We've got to get in the air before people start wondering what's happening out here on the lake at night."

"I'm not crazy about riding in this thing if something's busted."

"You checked those floats yourself."

With that, the pilot started the engine again. The boat had glided forward so there was again a little slack in the anchor rope, but the pilot began to work the plane forward nervously as the engine revved up. There was no noticeable jerk when he opened the throttle.

The plane struggled valiantly against the weight of the boat. The motor roared, and the light craft lurched to one side as the sluggish flat-bottomed scow surged in that direction.

"Felicia, we've got to get out of here! We'll be killed!" Joan warned.

Before the Cartright girl could answer, the pilot cut the motor. The plane stopped once more, abruptly. The boat continued to move forward until it jerked the tail of the plane again as it came to the end of the anchor rope.

Instantly the doors on either side of the plane flew open.

"I tell you, there's something wrong!" the pilot shouted. By this time, there was fear in his voice.

"Felt to me just like a car does when you go to pull another one, boss," Pete said, "the way it jerked."

"I suppose we're towing another plane!" the pilot snapped.

"Something's sure haywire." The girls could hear him climb down on the float again. "Give me that flashlight. I think we're dragging something."

Joan slipped out of her shoes. Felicia saw what she was doing and followed suit. They had only moved one hundred yards or so offshore.

Pete took the flashlight and sent its yellow beam along the fuselage. He cursed loudly.

"I told you that we were pulling something, boss! There's a boat back here with the anchor rope thrown over the tail."

"A boat?"

"That's what I said. The anchor's hooked onto the tail. Looks like it's torn the fabric!"

They were so interested in the plane and the damage done to it that they didn't think to throw their light on the boat.

"Let me see!" The pilot crawled out of the plane onto the other float. "If that tail section is damaged, we're in trouble. Bad trouble."

Pete moved toward the back of the float. As he did so, the flashlight beam bobbed erratically around to rest momentarily on the boat. The girls froze as the yellow beam transfixed them.

"Pete!" the pilot cried. "Shine that light on the boat again!"

"It's those blasted girls! We might have known they would be up to something!"

"This time we'll fix them good!" There was a dark threat in his voice.

"That's what we should have done back in the cottage! If we had, we'd be out of here by now."

"Are you ready, Joan?" Felicia whispered.

"That water's going to be awfully cold."

"It's our only chance."

"Wendy wasn't tied," the Bailey girl said. "Do you think she'll know to jump?"

"I was wondering the same thing."

"I'm going to get those girls," Pete retorted. "You get the anchor off the tail."

"I'm giving the orders around here!"

"Jump!" Joan cried.

As she spoke, she and Felicia dove into the icy water. The shock of the cold water slammed the breath out of them. Felicia felt her arms and legs go numb, and for a moment, she feared she would not be able to swim. But she kept plowing on, desperately.

"Oh, no, you don't!" they heard the pilot shout. "If you know what's good for you, you'll stay right in that plane!"

But he must have been too late. They heard a resounding splash as Wendy leaped out of the plane into the lake.

"Get her!" the pilot cried. "Get her!"

"You blasted kid!" Pete shouted. "Come back here!"

CHAPTER 14

DECISIONS ARE REACHED, ONE MOST IMPORTANT

Joan Bailey was a powerful swimmer. She reached shore and was just pulling herself from the water when a huge searchlight flashed on to sweep the lake until it caught the plane and bathed it in a dazzling, blinding light.

"This is the police!" a stern voice shouted from the dock. "Don't make a move! We've got you covered!"

"We haven't done anything!" the pilot protested. "What do you want?"

"Keep those hands up! We're coming!"

"Ask them what they've done with my daughter?" Judge Adams told the police.

"Listen, you two! Where's the girl?"

"What girl?"

About that time, Felicia reached shore. She got to her feet shakily. The water had seemed cold enough, but the chilly air seemed even colder. Her lips were blue and her teeth chattering.

The little knot of people was so concerned about the plane and the officers that they didn't even see Joan and Felicia. They didn't hear Wendy either as she swam onto the shore a moment or two later.

"Wendy!" Felicia cried, hurrying over to her. "Are you all right?"

At the sound of his daughter's name, the judge whirled. "Wendy? Are you there?"

The tall girl almost ran into his arms, wet and sobbing her relief.

"Oh, Dad!" she said over and over again. "It was so terrible. Those men were going to kidnap me."

He put his arm around her comfortingly.

"Everything's going to be all right."

She shuddered.

"I thought you would never come."

Then she remembered Joan and Felicia, and there they were!

"If it hadn't been for these girls," she said, "I don't know what I'd have done. Those men were going to fly me to some secret hideout, and they'd have done it if Felicia and Joan hadn't stopped them."

"If it's all the same to you," Joan said, her teeth chattering, "I'd just as soon c-c-c-continue this conversation after I g-g-get warm and into some dry clothes."

"Me, too," Wendy said, laughing almost hysterically.

"Come and get into the car," Judge Adams said. "Mom is at the house."

"But what about those two men?" Wendy asked fearfully. "What's going to happen to them?"

"The sheriff and his deputies will take care of them. They aren't going to cause you, or anybody else, any trouble for a long while."

The judge took the girls to the house. Mrs. Adams came running out and swept Wendy into her arms.

"You found her!" she sobbed. "You found her! You found her!"

"These girls found her," Judge Adams corrected. "But now you'd better let them get warm and into dry clothes, or we're likely to have three cases of pneumonia."

They each took a warm shower and slipped into dry clothing and a robe.

"Wendy," Mrs. Adams said when they finally came back into the living room, "when we got here and saw everything overturned and then read that note, we were terrified. Those men were so desperate that they would have done anything."

The judge nodded.

"So many strange things have happened that we couldn't figure out what was going on. But we knew that it was something serious."

"I probably shouldn't have left," her father went on, "but I felt that I had to be absolutely fair to Gallardo. So we got away for a few days, so I'd have an opportunity to study the evidence and be sure there is just cause for allowing the trial to continue."

"But everybody knows that he's guilty, Dad," Wendy protested. "Why do you have to give him that sort of consideration?"

"A lot of people ask that, my dear," he answered slowly, "but we can never run roughshod over the rights of an individual. Those safeguards are basic, designed to assure an innocent man the right of freedom."

"What are you going to do about Rocky Gallardo now?" his daughter asked. "Are you going to set him free for lack of evidence?"

His face grew solemn. "I can assure you this much. The note those men left and what they did will be introduced into the trial as evidence. On the basis of developments so far, I wouldn't advise Mr. Rocky Gallardo to plan any extended vacation. I rather imagine that his future is going to be quite well mapped out for him. But don't quote me. I'm talking now as a father, not as a judge."

Mrs. Adams fixed hot chocolate, and they drank it hungrily.

"Dad," Wendy said, getting back to the subject once more, "what would you have done if the girls hadn't helped me to get away? Would you have set Gallardo free?"

His thin lips narrowed.

"That's an unfair question, Wendy," he answered.

"This doesn't mean that I don't love you, but there are times when a man's duty must stand ahead of any personal problem."

She went to him impulsively and kissed him on the forehead. "I'm proud of you, Dad. That's what I kept telling those men."

The girls then went to bed exhausted.

"I don't know why I'm going to bed," Joan said, "I don't think I'll be able to sleep. Such a night!"

"It turned out a great deal happier than I thought."

"You can say that again."

Felicia sat beside the bed for a moment.

"All of these things in the past few days fit into the pattern now, don't they?" she said. "Wendy told me that Pete was the guy who peeked in her window at Wellington. I suppose he got a job there for a few days just to watch her."

"That's how he knew that we went to her hometown for the weekend, I suppose." Joan took a deep breath. "But it doesn't explain why they broke into the house in town and again out here and tore the papers up the way they did."

"While you were taking your shower, Judge Adams explained about that. He said that he is convinced they were going through his papers in an effort to find something crooked that he was doing. One of the gang approached him a few days ago and warned him that they were going over his life with a microscope, and when they got evidence of a crooked deal, he was going to play ball with Gallardo or they'd ruin him."

"And when they couldn't find any evidence of cheating or dishonesty on Judge Adams' part," Joan put in, "I suppose they decided that they would have to kidnap Wendy if they were going to be able to make him do what they wanted him to do."

"That's what he figured."

"It does all fit together."

They were still talking when there was a light knock on the door and Wendy Adams came in.

"I saw your light on, and I knew that you were still up," she explained.

"I'm really too tense to go to sleep for a while," Joan said.

"I can't sleep either." Wendy's youthful face was somber. "But that's not the reason."

The two girls looked at her.

"I'm sorry that I have treated you the way I have," she continued. "I've been terribly rude."

"Don't think a thing of it," Felicia answered. "We don't."

"Especially tonight." She sat down and was wringing her hands nervously. "I wanted to go to church with you this evening. Honestly, I did. But to be frank with you, I was afraid."

"Why, Wendy?" the Cartright girl insisted softly.

"You know."

"The Holy Spirit won't always speak to you the

way He has been speaking to you, Wendy," she said. "Why don't you give your heart to Him?"

"That's the thing that's almost driven me crazy the last few days!" The old belligerence came back to her voice momentarily. "I want to become a Christian. You'll never know how wicked and unclean I feel right now. How much I want to be saved! But it doesn't fit in with my plans. I've got my life all mapped out. And I know I couldn't do what I want to do and be a Christian."

Joan Bailey nodded sympathetically.

"Did you ever think that maybe you ought to change your plans?" she asked. "No plan is better for your life or will bring you any more happiness than God's plan for you. Why don't you put your trust in Him and let Him have His way? You'll never regret it."

Her gaze bored into theirs.

"Do you honestly believe that?"

"I know that it's true," Joan said. "I've proved it. I've found it out for myself."

"And so have I," Felicia added. "That's one reason we've been so concerned about you. It's the only way that any of us can hope to be truly happy." She paused. "But, Wendy, you're the only one who can settle the matter. I can't do it for you. Your parents can't do it for you, and neither can Joan. You are the one who must recognize that you are a sinner. You are the one who will suffer if you do not accept Him as your Savior."

"But, Felicia!" she protested miserably. "I can't go on the way I have been. I want to become a Christian!"

Joan got down the Bible. Together the girls began to explain the way of salvation.

* * *

Back at Wellington School for Girls the next week, the others noticed that something had happened to Wendy.

"What did you do to her, Joan?" one of them asked incredulously.

"Why?"

"I told my roommate that you must have pulled her fangs. She's sweet and a lot of fun. We like her."

"The thing that happened to change her was in a way simple."

Her companion's eyes questioned her. "Don't tell me that she's got religion."

"I wouldn't say that she 'got' anything," Felicia put in. "She accepted Jesus Christ as her personal Savior. That's why she's so different."

The girl stared.

"Now you've got me curious. I'm going to have to come up to your room sometime and find out what it's all about."

Wendy stepped out of the shadows. "I'd like to tell you," she said, smiling, "if I may."

"Wendy!" the girl exclaimed, blushing furiously. "Now I am embarrassed. Did you hear what I said?"

"I didn't mean to be eavesdropping," she answered, "but I did hear what you said. I think it's one of the nicest things anyone has said to me or about me since I've been here. You see, I've been praying sincerely that God would give me the strength to be truer, sweeter, and more agreeable. I want my testimony to count for my Lord."

The other girl's eyes appeared large and luminous. "What do you mean, *testimony?*"

By this time several girls had gathered.

"Why don't you come with me to my room?" Wendy said, taking her arm. "I'd like to tell you about it."

Felicia and Joan looked at one another. Their eyes filled with tears as they walked away in silence.

THE
FELICIA CARTRIGHT
SERIES

Felicia Cartright, a petite blonde who is one of the most popular students at Wellington School for Girls, has a surprising inclination toward mysteries. If a mysterious situation arises, it either makes its way to Felicia, or Felicia somehow finds it. Though this is a bit trying for her happy-go-lucky roommate, Joan Bailey, it does prevent life from becoming monotonous. It also enables Bernard Palmer, the popular author of the "Danny Orlis" books, to write an entertaining series of stories for girls aged twelve to eighteen.

The mysteries range from a valuable missing antique to an attempt by claim jumpers to steal a deposit of tungsten ore. There's excitement and action galore—but there's also spiritual guidance and blessing because Felicia and her partner-in-adventure love the Lord and take Him into account in all their experiences.

AVAILABLE FROM WWW.ANEKOPRESS.COM